SEATED

Living from Our Position in Christ

DONNA GAINES

NavPress

Discipleship Inside Out™

NAVPRESS

Discipleship Inside Out™

NavPress is the publishing ministry of The Navigators, an international Christian organization and leader in personal spiritual development. NavPress is committed to helping people grow spiritually and enjoy lives of meaning and hope through personal and group resources that are biblically rooted, culturally relevant, and highly practical.

For a free catalog go to www.NavPress.com
or call 1.800.366.7788 in the United States or 1.800.839.4769 in Canada.

ISBN-13: 978-1-61747-163-6

Cover design by Arvid Wallen
Cover photo by Yezepchyk Oleksandr/Shutterstock

Some of the anecdotal illustrations in this book are true to life and are included with the permission of the persons involved. All other illustrations are composites of real situations, and any resemblance to people living or dead is coincidental.

Unless otherwise identified, all Scripture quotations in this publication are taken from the New American Standard Bible® (NASB), Copyright © 1960, 1962, 1963, 1968, 1971, 1972, 1973, 1975, 1977, 1995 by The Lockman Foundation. Used by permission. Other versions used include: *THE MESSAGE* (MSG). Copyright © 1993, 1994, 1995, 1996, 2000, 2001, 2002. Used by permission of NavPress Publishing Group; the *Holy Bible, New Living Translation* (NLT), copyright © 1996. Used by permission of Tyndale House Publishers, Inc., Wheaton, Illinois 60189. All rights reserved; the *Amplified Bible* (AMP), © The Lockman Foundation 1954, 1958, 1962, 1964, 1965, 1987; and the *Holy Bible, New International Version®* (NIV®), Copyright © 1973, 1978, 1984 by International Bible Society, used by permission of Zondervan, all rights reserved.

Printed in the United States of America

1 2 3 4 5 6 7 8 / 15 14 13 12 11

This book is lovingly dedicated to my parents,
Dempsey and Joyce Dodds,
for living out the gospel before your children,
grandchildren, and now great-grandchildren.
I love you!

Seated

Seated in the heavenlies
That is where we are.
Carry us unto the place
Where the seat won't seem so far.
Show us how to love You more,
Jesus, Saviour, great Lover of our souls.

He raised us up.
He seated us by grace not of ourselves.
A gift from God,
He raised us up.
He seated us.

Jesus, help us seek Your face
In all that we do,
So that everything we touch
Will be a touch from You.
This is why we need Your grace.
Lord, remind us of our heavenly place.

— CHARLOTTE GUFFIN

CONTENTS

ACKNOWLEDGMENTS

TO MY BELOVED SISTERS in Christ, the women of Bellevue Baptist Church, for the honor of serving our Lord alongside each of you. What a joy it is to study God's Word with you! Thank you, Marge Lenow, for your leadership in our women's ministry and for always being open to the movement and direction of the Holy Spirit. Special thanks to Dayna Street for all of your help with the workbook. Your creativity inspires me—thank you for your friendship!

Thank you, Mike Miller and Marsha Pursley, for your encouragement. Since my college days, The Navigators has greatly impacted my life for Christ. Your Bible studies and *Topical Memory System* challenged me to know Christ more intimately through His Word. Thank you for the honor of publishing with you.

Thank you to my husband, Steve, for supporting me as I seek to follow God's leadership. Your encouragement and belief in God's call challenge me to keep stepping out in faith. To my parents, thank you for your unconditional love and support. And to my children and grandchildren, may you always walk in the truth!

To my Lord and Savior, Jesus Christ, be all glory and honor and power!

HOW TO USE THIS STUDY

THIS STUDY IS MEANT to be a combination of personal study throughout the week followed by a group meeting once a week. Each session's personal study is divided into four days, which will each require approximately thirty minutes of your time. On these four days you will be asked to read Scripture passages, answer various questions about how the passages apply to your life, take some time to meditate upon what you've learned, and write down any further thoughts you might have.

During your weekly small-group time, you will watch a video that supplements the personal study you've already done. As you watch the video, please take notes on the Listening Guide pages included in this workbook and write down any questions you might have. After watching the video, you will have plenty of time to discuss both the video and the personal study with your small group. Finally, you will have opportunities to pray for yourself and the other members of your small group.

INTRODUCTION

WELCOME TO THIS STUDY on the book of Ephesians! Ephesians is an instruction manual for living life as God intended—seated with Christ. Throughout the next few weeks you will discover who you are in Christ and the blessings you have inherited through His death and resurrection. The truths in this study, if applied, will radically alter how you think, live, and relate.

You will:

- Discover who you are in Christ
- Learn how to take charge of your thoughts and control your emotions
- Grasp God's design for Spirit-filled relationships
- Be equipped to stand against the schemes Satan uses to defeat you

We have a new identity as joint heirs with Christ. So often substandard Christianity prevents us from experiencing all that is available to believers. It is time to take our seat in Christ Jesus!

God, being rich in mercy, because of His great love with which He loved us, even when we were dead in our transgressions, made us alive together with Christ (by grace you have been saved), and raised us up with Him, and seated us with Him in the heavenly places in Christ Jesus.

—EPHESIANS 2:4-6

INTRODUCTION LISTENING GUIDE

1. **The Setting: Ephesus**

   "Ephesus was 'the' religious center of the province of Asia. The great temple of Artemis there drew tourists and worshipers, and served as a giant bank from which cities and nations as well as individuals applied for loans. This highly successful institutionalized religion is the backdrop against which Paul gives us a vision of the church of Jesus Christ. This church is no institution: it is a body, a family, a holy but living temple. It reveals a glory in the living personalities of its members which far outshines the glory of the stone temple of Ephesus, even though that temple was four times the size of the Parthenon of Athens."[1]

2. **The Author: Paul**

   It is thought that Paul wrote his letter to the Ephesians from a Roman prison around AD 60–62. A man named Tychicus delivered it to the Ephesian church. This book is one of Paul's five prison epistles (Ephesians, Philippians, Colossians, Philemon, and 2 Timothy).

3. **The Saints**

   We are chosen.

   We are predestined through Jesus Christ.

   - Am I chosen or free?
       Acts 16:31
       John 1:12

Ephesians 1:13

Romans 8:28-29

- Did Jesus die for all?

    Romans 5:18

    2 Corinthians 5:14,19

    1 Timothy 2:3-4

    2 Peter 2:1

    2 Peter 3:9

    1 John 2:2

    Hebrews 2:9

- Is it possible to reject Christ?

    Matthew 23:37

    Matthew 11:20

    Luke 7:30

    Acts 7:51

- Is it possible to lose your salvation?

    John 5:24

    John 6:39-40

    John 10:27-30

    Romans 8:16

    Hebrews 10:14

- This system of beliefs can be summed up like this:

    T—Total Depravity

    U—Unconditional Election

    L—Limited Atonement

    I—Irresistible Grace

    P—Perseverance of the Saints

We must **sit**. Then we will have the ability to **walk**
and the power to **stand**!

BLESSED!

Ephesians 1

How blessed is God! And what a blessing he is! He's the Father of our Master, Jesus Christ, and takes us to the high places of blessing in him. Long before he laid down earth's foundations, he had us in mind, had settled on us as the focus of his love, to be made whole and holy by his love.

—EPHESIANS 1:3-4 (MSG)

THE WORD *BLESSING* IS often tossed about in Christian circles, but what does the word really mean? What does the Bible say about blessings? And what blessings has God given to all believers? As you study the first chapter of the book of Ephesians you will discover the answers to these questions. God has blessed us with more than we can ever know or imagine, and we can get a glimpse of His blessings by what Paul described to the church in Ephesus.

Before you dive in, take several minutes to be still and pray. Ask God to work in your heart as you search His Word. Ask Him to reveal to you the things He wants you to learn. Thank Him for the blessings He has given you. And praise Him for being such a great and glorious God!

Day 1: A Greeting *(Ephesians 1:1-2)*
Paul wrote under the authority of the Father and the Son.

Day 2: A Doxology of Praise and Blessing *(Ephesians 1:3-14)*
God is the source of all blessings.

Day 3: Thanksgiving and Prayer *(Ephesians 1:15-23)*
Obedience to Christ's authority will result in transformation.

Day 4: Practical Application *(Ephesians 1:1-23)*
We are blessed!

DAY ONE

A GREETING

Ephesians 1:1-2

Praise, my soul, the King of Heaven;
To His feet thy tribute bring!
Ransomed, healed, restored, forgiven,
Who like me His praise should sing?
Praise Him! Praise Him!
Praise the everlasting King!

— HENRY FRANCIS LYTE (1793–1847)

Key Point:

Paul wrote under the authority of the Father and the Son.

PAUL FIRST VISITED THE city of Ephesus on his second missionary journey, accompanied by Priscilla and Aquila, whom he left there to continue the ministry (see Acts 18:18-19). Paul returned to Ephesus on his third missionary journey and stayed for approximately three years (see Acts 19; 20:31). During those years, Ephesus was essentially an evangelistic center, as Paul sent various missionaries from there to the outlying areas of Asia Minor. When Paul left the city a final time, he left his disciple Timothy to continue to lead the church.

The city of Ephesus, the capital of the Roman province of Asia, was a major coastal intersection located on the Aegean Sea. At the time of Paul's visits, the population was likely around 250,000, which made it the fourth or fifth largest city in the Roman Empire.[1] Due to its size and strategic location, Ephesus was an important commercial, educational, and political center in the world at the time.

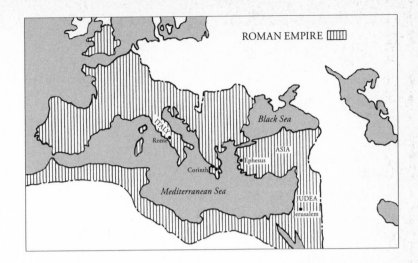

A major source of income for Ephesus was the temple of Diana, the fertility goddess. The temple was built completely of marble, was four times the size of the Parthenon, took 220 years to build, and was one of the seven wonders of the ancient world. Thousands of worshipers visited this temple each year, bringing a large amount of income to the businesses in Ephesus. Warren Wiersbe wrote, "Paul's letter to the Ephesians is as carefully structured as that great temple of Diana, and it contains greater beauty and wealth! We inherit the wealth by faith and invest the wealth by works. Without the spiritual balance, our spiritual riches do us no good."[2]

> Paul's letter to the Ephesians is as carefully structured as that great temple of Diana, and it contains greater beauty and wealth!
> — WARREN WIERSBE

Paul opened his letter to the Ephesians with a doxology of praise to God for the true eternal blessings He lavishes upon those who worship Him. As you journey throughout this study, be on the lookout for the many spiritual riches God has granted all believers. The first chapter of Ephesians overflows with these blessings!

Read Ephesians 1:1-2. Paul wrote the book of Ephesians around AD 61 while he was under house arrest in Rome (see Acts 28:16-31). Because the book was actually written as a letter, Paul opened with a greeting to his brothers and sisters in Christ.

1. How did Paul identify himself to the church at Ephesus? *(verse 1)*

2. From whose authority did Paul speak? *(verses 1-2)*

Paul reminded the people of Ephesus that he was an apostle of Jesus, but more importantly, he said he was an apostle only by the will of God. He made it clear that he spoke not from his own authority, power, or wisdom but from the authority of both God the Father and the Son. In doing so, he pointed out that Jesus is equal to God the Father.

3. What word did Paul use to describe the saints at Ephesus? *(verse 1)*

Ephesians is addressed to "the saints . . . who are faithful." From this we can deduct that Paul was not writing to correct disobedience (as he was in other letters) but to instruct his readers in the blessings they had inherited from Christ.

In our translations of Scripture, we read that this letter is to the faithful saints "at Ephesus." However, the words "at Ephesus" were not included in the earliest manuscripts of the book of Ephesians that still exist today. Most scholars believe Ephesians was written as an encyclical letter that was sent originally to the church in Ephesus with the intention that it then be circulated throughout several churches. As the letter traveled from church to church, the blank could be filled in with the name of each church as it was being read.

4. With what words did Paul greet the believers? *(verse 2)*

Paul often wrote the words *grace* and *peace* in his greeting to believers (see Romans 1:7; 1 Corinthians 1:3; 2 Corinthians 1:2; Galatians 1:3; Colossians 1:2). By using these two words, Paul combined the common Jewish greeting *shalom* (peace) with the traditional Gentile greeting *charis* (grace). With his statement in verse 2 Paul declared that the grace and peace he wished for the Ephesians were blessings from the Lord.

5. In what ways do we greet fellow believers? How do they compare with Paul's greeting?

FURTHER THOUGHTS:

A DOXOLOGY OF PRAISE AND BLESSING

Ephesians 1:3-14

IF WE WERE TO read from the original Greek manuscripts, Ephesians 1:3-14 would be one long sentence. In fact, it is the longest sentence that has ever been found in an ancient Greek manuscript. This kind of sentence is known as a *berakah*, a form of praise based on Hebrew psalms and hymns often used in Jewish liturgy. In these verses, Paul not only praised God but also began to outline the blessings God has for His children.

Read Ephesians 1:3-14.

1. Paul began his *berakah* by directing the blessing toward God. Why did Paul say God was worthy of blessing and praise? *(verse 3)*

God is worthy of our blessing and praise because *He* has blessed *us* with every spiritual blessing! The phrase *spiritual blessing* does not mean that God's blessings are only to be found in the spiritual realm; we receive many material blessings from Him as well. Rather, it means that all blessings have a spiritual source—God.

2. What additional reasons did Paul give for honoring God with blessing? *(verse 4)*

God not only chose us, but He also decreed that we should be "holy and blameless" (verse 4). We bless God for taking us from sin and death to holiness and new life.

3. What has God predestined believers to become? *(verse 5)*

In Paul's day, most adoptions took place because families lacked a male heir to inherit their land and carry on the family name. Therefore, adoptive fathers took great care to choose men of good character to fulfill this role. Contrast that to our predestination to be adopted as God's sons and daughters. God has chosen both men and women, with all of our various sins and character flaws, to be "heirs of God and fellow heirs with Christ" (Romans 8:17) if we believe in Christ. The *Ryrie Study Bible* notes:

> God has determined beforehand that those who believe in Christ will be adopted into His family and conformed to His Son. It involves a choice on His part (v. 4); it is based on the good pleasure of His perfect will (vv. 5, 9, 11); its purpose is to glorify God (v. 14); but it does not relieve man of his responsibility to believe the gospel in order to bring to pass personally God's predestination (v. 13).[3]

It is extremely important to note that while God has predestined us, we still have a personal responsibility for our salvation. Many take the idea of predestination to mean that we can just sit back and do nothing—that if we were meant to be saved, then we will be. Others have taken this even further by declaring that if God predestines people, we need not share the gospel. However, this is not what the whole of Scripture reveals.

> God has determined beforehand that those who believe in Christ will be adopted into His family . . . but it does not relieve man of his responsibility to believe the gospel in order to bring to pass personally God's predestination.
> — *Ryrie Study Bible*

In his book *The Knowledge of the Holy*, A. W. Tozer wrote,

In this utter dependence of all things upon the creative will of God lies the possibility for both holiness and sin. One of the marks of God's image in man is his ability to exercise moral choice. The teaching of Christianity is that man chose to be independent of God and confirmed his choice by deliberately disobeying a divine command. This act violated the relationship that normally existed between God and His creature; it rejected God as the ground of existence and threw man back upon himself.[4]

In other words, we do have a personal responsibility and the ability to exercise our moral choice.

4. In verses 7-9, Paul listed three blessings believers have in Jesus Christ:

a. _____ through His blood *(verse 7)*

b. The _____ of our trespasses *(verse 7)*

c. Knowledge of the _____ of His will . . . which He purposed in Christ *(verse 9)*

While these are by no means the extent of God's blessings to us, the other blessings mean nothing without them. We are redeemed (released from our debt through payment of a ransom), forgiven (pardoned), and given the knowledge of the mystery of reconciliation with God.

5. At "the fullness of the times" what two things will be placed under the authority of Jesus Christ? *(verse 10)*

When Paul wrote "the fullness of the times" in verse 10, he was referring to the end times that will occur at a time known only to God. At that time, a new heaven and a new earth will be completely unified under the rule of Christ.

6. **Read Deuteronomy 4:20 and 9:29.** How did Moses refer to the nation of Israel?

In Ephesians 1:11-12, Paul used the pronoun "we" as he included himself with the other Jewish believers who would receive an inheritance in Christ and who were the first to hope in Him. Because the pronoun "we" in verses 11-12 referred to Jewish believers, the words "you also" in verse 13 identified the Gentiles (non-Jews) who had heard the truth of the gospel message and believed.

7. With what are all believers—both Jew and Gentile—sealed? *(verse 13)*

Regarding the word *seal*, the *Ryrie Study Bible* notes: "A seal indicated possession and security. The presence of the Holy Spirit, the seal, is the believer's guarantee of the security of his salvation."[5] This seal—the Holy Spirit—is a pledge (verse 14), which could also be translated *deposit* or *guarantee*. The word was used to describe a down payment that ensured a buyer would one day return and pay the full amount.

> He who establishes us with you in Christ and anointed us is God, who also sealed us and gave us the Spirit in our hearts as a pledge.
> — 2 CORINTHIANS 1:21-22

8. Does the understanding of the Holy Spirit as a seal change your view of this person of the Trinity? In what way?

FURTHER THOUGHTS:

THANKSGIVING AND PRAYER

Ephesians 1:15-23

Key Point:

Obedience to Christ's authority will result in transformation.

IN EPHESIANS 1:3-14, PAUL offered his thanksgiving and praise to God. In verses 15-23, Paul verbalized his thanks for his readers and wrote a prayer for them. Within this prayer, we discover more blessings and learn about Christ's authority. Like verses 3-14, verses 15-23 are also one continuous sentence in the Greek. They are to be considered as one thought.

Read Ephesians 1:15-23.

1. Paul continued his letter by assuring his readers that he was continually praying for them. What two things had Paul heard about the believers in the church at Ephesus? *(verses 15-16)*

a.

b.

2. What did Paul ask God to give to this group of believers? *(verse 17)*

Wisdom is the ability to see life from God's point of view. *Revelation* is insight into the mysteries of God.

3. Why do you think Paul asked God to give his readers these two traits?

4. Paul continued his prayer for the saints in verses 18-19. As he prayed, he asked God to enlighten them with three realities. List them below.

    a.

    b.

    c.

> I pray that the eyes of your heart may be enlightened, so that you will know what is the hope of His calling, what are the riches of the glory of His inheritance in the saints, and what is the surpassing greatness of His power toward us who believe. These are in accordance with the working of the strength of His might.
> — EPHESIANS 1:18-19

As the eyes of our hearts are enlightened, true spiritual formation begins to take place from the inside out. We start to understand the greatness of the blessings God has given us, and those blessings change us. In his book *Holy Available*, Gary Thomas described this process: "The more clearly we see, the more faithfully we obey. The more we obey, the more clearly we will see, and — over time — the more deeply we will mirror the spirit and life and character of Christ."[6]

> The more clearly we see, the more faithfully we obey. The more we obey, the more clearly we will see, and — over time — the more deeply we will mirror the spirit and life and character of Christ. — GARY THOMAS

In verses 20-23, Paul acknowledged that this spiritual transformation takes place only through the resurrection power of Jesus Christ. The power that raised Him from the dead is the same power that transforms our lives.

5. Where is Christ right now? *(verse 20)*

6. Describe the authority that God has given to Christ. *(verses 21-23)*

7. Who is the head of the church? *(verse 22)*

8. How did Paul describe the church? *(verse 23)*

We read that Jesus is the head of the church and that the believers are His body. He has all authority, yet He does not use His power for selfish measures. Instead, Christ's rule is based on service to His church.

FURTHER THOUGHTS:

DAY FOUR

PRACTICAL APPLICATION

Ephesians 1:1-23

Read Ephesians 1:1-23 again. How blessed we are in Christ! Yet we often get so wrapped up in the struggles, the busyness, and the demands of our own lives that we forget to bless God for the

Key Point:

We are blessed!

many ways He has blessed us. More than forgetfulness, this is actually neglectfulness.

1. **Read Psalm 103:1-5.** Make a list of God's benefits toward us.

2. List five specific ways you have seen God's hand of blessing in your life during this past week.

    a.

    b.

    c.

    d.

    e.

3. How can *you* be a blessing? Create a blessing plan for this week. Determine three ways you can be a blessing to someone else, and then do it! In the space below, record the specific ways you blessed someone.

In Psalm 103:2, David wrote, "Bless the LORD, O my soul, and forget none of His benefits." Throughout the book of Ephesians, we are reminded of the benefits of Christ. Below is a chart titled "Benefits in Christ." As you study the book of Ephesians each week, circle the phrases that include the words "in Christ," "in the Beloved," and so on. Use the chart to record those benefits.

Benefits in Christ	Scripture Reference

FURTHER THOUGHTS:

SESSION 1 LISTENING GUIDE

BLESSED!

Ephesians 1

What comes into our minds when we think about God is the most important thing about us.

—A. W. TOZER

1. **We Are Blessed** *(verses 3-16)*
   To be blessed means "to prosper" or "to declare that we are indwelt by God, and thereby we should be fully satisfied." We are blessed:

   - By the _____ (verses 3-6)
   - Through the _____ (verses 7-12)
   - In the _____ (verses 13-14)

2. **Paul's Prayer** *(verses 15-17)*
   Wisdom:

   Revelation:

3. **Our Inheritance** *(verses 18-23)*

    1. Every spiritual blessing *(verse 3)*

    2. Chosen to be holy and blameless *(verse 4)*

    3. Predestined to adoption *(verses 5-6)*

    4. Redemption through His blood *(verse 7)*

    5. Forgiveness of sins *(verse 7)*

    6. Revelation of the mystery *(verse 9)*

    7. Hope that leads to praise *(verse 12)*

    8. Marked with a seal *(verse 13)*

    9. Power of His mighty strength *(verses 19-20)*

   10. Seated in Christ—given authority *(verse 20)*

4. **What Is Real?**

Righteous in Christ

Evangelistic, encouraging, enthusiastic

Authentic

Loving

> *God is most glorified in us when*
> *we are most satisfied in Him.*
> —JOHN PIPER[8]

ALIVE!

Ephesians 2

God saved you by his special favor when you believed. And you can't take credit for this; it is a gift from God. Salvation is not a reward for the good things we have done, so none of us can boast about it.

— EPHESIANS 2:8-9 (NLT)

JUST AS A PHYSICALLY dead man is completely devoid of any sign of life, so a spiritually dead man exhibits no indications of spiritual life. Paul observed in Ephesians 2:1, "Once you were dead, doomed forever because of your many sins"(NLT). How do we escape the graveyard of spiritual doom? Only by the grace of God! Speaking of this passage from spiritual death to life, Warren Wiersbe wrote, "What a miracle of God's grace! We are taken out of a graveyard of sin and placed into the throne room of glory."[1] No more stench of death, no more graveclothes; we have been transformed from degenerate to regenerate. By His grace we are alive!

Day 1: The State of Sinful Humanity *(Ephesians 2:1-3)*
We were dead in sin.

Day 2: The Source of New Life *(Ephesians 2:4-10)*
We have new life in Christ.

Day 3: The Reality of Unity *(Ephesians 2:11-22)*
We are united in Christ.

Day 4: Practical Application *(Ephesians 2)*
We are alive!

DAY ONE

THE STATE OF SINFUL HUMANITY

Ephesians 2:1-3

What is grace? How would you define it? Probably the most popular two-word definition is "unmerited favor." To amplify that a bit: Grace is what God does for mankind, which we do not deserve, which we cannot earn, and which we will never be able to repay. Awash in our sinfulness, helpless to change on our own, polluted to the core with no possibility of cleaning ourselves up, we cry out for grace.

—CHARLES R. SWINDOLL

Key Point:

We were dead in sin.

THE SECOND CHAPTER OF Ephesians doesn't start on a happy note, but Paul wasn't known for sugarcoating the message; he was known for stating the truth. And the reality is that without Christ, we are doomed. Although today's verses focus only on death, rest assured that Paul first told us we are dead in sin so that we can better understand the glorious life we receive through Jesus.

Read Ephesians 2:1.

1. What word did Paul use to depict man?

2. How would you describe someone who is physically dead?

The word *trespasses* in verse 1 implies slipping into sin, while the word *sins* refers to man's inherent disposition toward evil. Both words indicate deliberate acts against God, which result in man's inability to live a life pleasing to God. The plural use of both words emphasizes man's bent toward a repetitive cycle of sin. The fruit of trespasses and sins is spiritual death reaped by those who are physically alive.

> You used to live just like the rest of the world, full of sin, obeying Satan, the mighty prince of the power of the air. He is the spirit at work in the hearts of those who refuse to obey God. All of us used to live that way, following the passions and desires of our evil nature. We were born with an evil nature, and we were under God's anger just like everyone else. – EPHESIANS 2:2-3 (NLT)

Read Ephesians 2:2-3 from the New Living Translation (see sidebar).

3. How did Paul describe our past lives? *(verses 2-3)*

4. Describe your own life before you knew Jesus. How does it compare to Paul's description?

While we all still sin even after we become believers, we no longer are "by nature children of wrath" (verse 3, NASB). Instead, we have been born again to a new life with Jesus, who we strive to obey and emulate.

5. When we live in sin, whom are we obeying? *(verse 2)*

Paul referred to the Devil as "the prince of the power of the air" (verse 2). This is a reminder that while Satan doesn't have ultimate power, he does still hold some power. In the *Women's Evangelical Commentary*, we read:

> The fleshly desires of people draw them to do evil things, and Satan and his demons work along with the world to draw them away from God. The flesh and Satan work as enemies of God's plan and design; therefore, those who have not accepted Christ as Savior are partners with the Devil. This thought is frightening but realistic.[2]

Indeed it is frightening, but it's also important to remind ourselves of the fact that Satan has not yet been fully crushed. He does still wield power, but we need not succumb to it.

FURTHER THOUGHTS:

DAY TWO

THE SOURCE OF NEW LIFE

Ephesians 2:4-10

AFTER PAUL REMINDED HIS readers that everyone was born into a life of sin and death, he revealed the antidote for the problem—redemption. Throughout history, the Jews had seen God redeem them from bad situation after bad situation. But they were still looking for that ultimate Redeemer—the King of kings and Lord of lords who would save them from the evil of this world.

Key Point:

We have new life in Christ.

Read Ephesians 2:4-10.

1. With the words, "But God," Paul began to unfold God's plan to redeem sinful man. What two attributes of God were displayed in His redemptive plan? *(verse 4)*

God didn't want us to receive the punishment we deserve because He loves us. It's that simple. We just need to accept His amazing mercy and love and acknowledge that redemption comes through Him. We should praise and bless Him every day for the gift of redemption. Take a look at A. W. Tozer's prayer in the margin. Pause for a few moments to pray that prayer yourself.

Holy Father, Thy wisdom excites our admiration, Thy power fills us with fear, Thy omnipresence turns every spot of earth into holy ground; but how shall we thank Thee enough for Thy mercy which comes down to the lowest part of our need to give us beauty for ashes, the oil of joy for mourning, and for the spirit of heaviness a garment of praise? We bless and magnify thy mercy, through Jesus Christ our Lord. Amen. – A. W. TOZER

2. In verses 5 and 6, what verbs did Paul use to contrast the "dead" lives of unbelievers with the lives of believers? Believers are:

a. _____ with Christ *(verse 5)*

b. _____ with Him *(verse 6)*

c. _____ with Him *(verse 6)*

Through our relationship with Jesus Christ, we, who were once dead in our sins, are now alive! As Romans 6:11 says, "Even so consider yourselves to be dead to sin, but alive to God in Christ Jesus." We read in Ephesians that we are not only alive with Him but also raised up with Him and seated with Him.

3. Look back at Ephesians 1:20. Where did Paul say Christ was seated?

4. Where did he say believers are seated? *(verse 6)*

We are seated with Christ. The Enemy is under His feet, and he is under our feet as well. We need to live from our position of being seated with Christ, where we are set free to love and serve and witness to the grace of God in our lives.

5. What reason did Paul give for God's redemptive action toward man? *(verse 7)*

6. In verse 8, Paul repeated his statement from Ephesians 2:5. By what means is man saved?

7. What word picture did Paul use to describe salvation? *(verse 8)*

The word *grace* is used more than 150 times in the New Testament. Paul used the word almost one hundred times himself, twelve of which were in Ephesians. Salvation by grace is the gift. Faith is the hand that receives the gift. And when we receive a gift, we thank the giver. In the space below, write a prayer of thanksgiving for God's gift of salvation to you.

8. In verses 8-9, Paul underscored the inability of man to do anything on his own about his sinful state. What reason did Paul give that God removed works from the salvation equation? *(verse 9)*

9. **Read Romans 11:6.** What did Paul say was the opposite of grace?

Warren Wiersbe said, "Salvation cannot be 'of works' because the work of salvation has already been completed on the cross. This is the work that God does for us, and it is a finished work. We can add nothing to it; we dare take nothing from it."[3] There is absolutely nothing we can do to earn our salvation. If there were, then what was the point of Jesus dying on the cross? As Elvina M. Hall said in her beloved hymn, "Jesus paid it all."[4] We pay nothing.

> Salvation cannot be "of works" because the work of salvation has already been completed on the cross. This is the work that God does for us, and it is a finished work. We can add nothing to it; we dare take nothing from it. — WARREN WIERSBE

10. What word did Paul use to describe believers? *(verse 10)*

The word *workmanship* refers to a masterpiece, a work of art. The psalmist wrote in Psalm 19:1, "The heavens declare the glory of God; and the firmament shows and proclaims His handiwork" (AMP). Although heaven and earth reflect the majesty of God in countless ways, God's greatest work — His most splendid masterpiece — is the one who becomes a new creature in Jesus Christ.

FURTHER THOUGHTS:

DAY THREE

THE REALITY OF UNITY

Ephesians 2:11-22

UNITY IN THE CHURCH is not just a modern-day issue. It has been around since the very beginning of the church. For two thousand years, the Jews and Gentiles had been in conflict, but now

Key Point:

We are united in Christ.

Paul was telling them they were united in Christ. That couldn't have been an easy idea for either group to embrace, but it was important for them to understand, as it still is for us today.

Read Ephesians 2:11-22. Most of the believers in the church at Ephesus were Gentiles. The Jews had always considered the Gentiles to be ceremonially unclean, but in these verses, Paul pointed out that both Jews and Gentiles were unclean until they were washed in the cleansing blood of the Lamb of God.

1. Who were the "Uncircumcision"? *(verse 11)*

2. Who were called the "Circumcision"? *(verse 11)*

3. In verse 12, Paul urged the Gentiles to remember what their lives were like before they knew Christ.

    a. They were _____ from Christ.

    b. They were _____ from the _____ of Israel.

c. They were _____ to the _____ of promise.

d. They had no _____.

e. They were _____ _____ in the world.

After he reminded the Gentiles of their past lives without Christ, Paul then detailed God's intervening plan on their behalf. He explained that now their lives were different in Christ.

4. How did God reconcile sinful man to Himself? *(verse 13)*

5. **Read Hebrews 9:22.** What did the writer of Hebrews give as the prerequisite for forgiveness?

6. What word is found four times in Ephesians 2:14-17?

7. The word *peace* can be defined as the absence of conflict and the presence of tranquility. What does it mean to you that "He Himself is our peace"? *(verse 14)*

8. What did Jesus abolish through His death? What did He establish? *(verse 15)*

9. What was the "one body" Paul referred to? *(verse 16)*

10. Christ came to preach to those who were _____
(the Gentiles) and to those who were _____ (the Jews).
(verse 17)

Through His death, Jesus broke down the walls of hostility that had existed between the Gentiles and the Jews, paving the way for peace between the two groups. Even more important, Christ's death made it possible for both to be reconciled to God.

11. What access are we granted through Jesus? *(verse 18)*

12. Paul told his Gentile brothers and sisters in Christ that they were no longer "strangers and aliens." By contrast, what did he say they were? *(verse 19)*

13. Paul called us "fellow citizens . . . of God's household" (verse 19). In what ways have you seen disunity among the citizens of God's household? In what ways can you strive to combat disunity within the church?

14. Paul wrote that "God's household" has a firm foundation—"the apostles and prophets." What metaphor did he use to describe Christ? *(verses 19-20)*

15. **Read Psalm 118:22-23, Isaiah 28:16, Matthew 21:42-43, and 1 Peter 2:4-10.** Record what you learn in these verses about Jesus being the chief corner stone.

16. As Paul concluded this chapter, he explained the ongoing work of God in the life of the believer. What is that continual work? *(verses 21-22)*

FURTHER THOUGHTS:

DAY FOUR

PRACTICAL APPLICATION

Ephesians 2

Key Point:

We are alive!

READ EPHESIANS 2 AGAIN. As you read through it, add items to your "Benefits in Christ" chart on page 30.

1. How has your life been changed since you were saved by grace through faith?

The word *remember* is used more than 150 times in the Bible. In Ephesians 2, Paul exhorted the believers to remember the difference their salvation by grace had made in their lives. In essence, Paul told them:

- **Remember** how you used to live a life without hope, **but now** you have hope!
- **Remember** when you were far away from God, **but now** God holds you close and you have direct access to Him!
- **Remember** you used to be strangers and aliens, **but now** you are a part of the family of God!

Take a few moments to reflect on the "Remember . . . but now" differences in your own life. Write them down in the chart on page 46.

Remember	But Now . . .

FURTHER THOUGHTS:

SESSION 2 LISTENING GUIDE

ALIVE!

Ephesians 2

It is, indeed, a marvel that, through these long ages of the world's wild wanderings, God should still follow His unworthy children with ceaseless love, never refusing to bless them, always entreating them to return to Him. . . . It is the nature of true and perfect love to be eternal.

—W. F. ADENEY

1. **We Were Pronounced Dead** *(verses 1-3)*
   We live in hostile territory.

   We must saturate our minds with the truth of God's Word.

2. **We Have Been Raised from the Dead** *(verses 4-7)*
   We are saved by God's great mercy.

   We are seated with Christ Jesus in heavenly places.

   We are on display—trophies of God's grace.

3. **We Are Saved by Grace Through Faith** *(verses 8-10)*
   Faith:

   Legalism:

We are God's masterpiece, created in Christ Jesus:

- Gender specific
- Temperament / Personality
  - Choleric / Lion
  - Sanguine / Otter
  - Melancholy / Beaver
  - Phlegmatic / Golden Retriever[5]
- Gifts
- Calling / Passion

4. **We Are Unified** *(verses 11-17)*
   Psalm 133

   Living in unity does not mean that we will agree on everything; there will be many opinions just as there are many notes in a musical chord. But we must agree on our purpose in life—to work together for God. Our outward expression of unity will reflect our inward unity of purpose.[6]

5. **We Are Built Up** *(verses 18-22)*
   1 Peter 2:4-6
   We are living stones that are being built up as the dwelling place of God's Spirit.

   Turn your eyes upon Jesus,
   Look full in His wonderful face
   And the things of earth will grow strangely dim
   In the light of His glory and grace.[7]

   —HELEN H. LEMMEL

UNCONTAINABLE!

Ephesians 3

To me, the very least of all saints, this grace was given, to preach to the Gentiles the unfathomable riches of Christ.

—Ephesians 3:8

THERE IS A DEEP longing within the heart of man to be connected to the heart of God. As that intimate connection occurs, God will begin to reveal His secrets to the one who is in pursuit of Him. Paul was a God-seeker. And in return, God made known to Paul the mystery of His Son and called Paul to a ministry that was uncontainable. As a result, Paul made a radical impact upon his world. God also wants our lives to be uncontainable!

Day 1: Paul Reveals the Mystery *(Ephesians 3:1-6)*
The gospel is for all people.

Day 2: Paul's Call to the Gentiles *(Ephesians 3:7-13)*
We do all things through God's power.

Day 3: Paul's Prayer for the Believers *(Ephesians 3:14-21)*
We are God's beloved.

Day 4: Practical Application *(Ephesians 3)*
God's call is uncontainable!

DAY ONE

PAUL REVEALS THE MYSTERY

Ephesians 3:1-6

It's an awesome secret: The call of God burning in your breast will be uncontainable and unstoppable as you devote yourself to the fiery passion of intimate communion with the Lover of your soul.

— BOB SORGE

Key Point:

The gospel is for all people.

PAUL BEGAN EPHESIANS 3 by explaining the mystery of Christ and his God-called ministry to share that mystery. Let's take a minute to explore Paul's usage of the word *mystery. The MacArthur New Testament Commentary* says, "Contrary to our use of *mystery* as a series of clues to be figured out, Paul's use of the word points to mystery as a heretofore unrevealed truth that has been made clear. The word *mystery* preserves the sense that the revealed truth has such awesome implications that it continues to amaze and humble those who accept it."[1] This is a bit different than our typical definition of mystery, so keep MacArthur's explanation in mind as you read Paul's words.

The word *mystery* preserves the sense that the revealed truth has such awesome implications that it continues to amaze and humble those who accept it. – JOHN MACARTHUR

Read Ephesians 3:1-5.

The first three words of chapter 3, "For this reason," refer back to the previous verses where Paul revealed that both Jews and Gentiles are united in Christ. Therefore, what he has to say here is directly related to this unity.

1. What did Paul disclose about himself? *(verse 1)*

Paul had been a Christian for about thirty years when he wrote his letter to the believers at Ephesus. Paul had been there on three missionary journeys during those years and had established churches throughout the Mediterranean. At the end of his third missionary trip, Paul was arrested in Jerusalem for inciting a riot while he was preaching. Caesar sent Paul to Rome, where he spent two years under house arrest. His house arrest was a minimum-security arrangement that allowed him to have visitors and send out letters. While under arrest at Rome, Paul wrote Ephesians, Colossians, Philippians, and Philemon.

2. In verses 2-4, Paul began to explain his ministry to the Gentiles. What had God called him to do?

Paul reiterated that it was God who had called him to this ministry. God commissioned Paul to use his gifts and abilities to share the mystery of Jesus Christ with both Jews and Gentiles. Of all people, Paul would have seemed the least likely person to preach to the Gentiles. After all, he was a self-proclaimed "Hebrew of Hebrews" and may have been a Pharisee (see Philippians 3:6). Yet God called him to reach out to those he would have formerly considered unclean.

3. This mystery had not been revealed to men in past generations. How was it being revealed now? *(verse 5)*

The Greek word for *mystery* is found approximately thirty times in the New Testament. Each time it refers to a mystery or secret. Stephen Renn wrote, "The underlying sense of this term in the majority of the contexts refers to that which has been kept a secret by God in the past, but which He has chosen to make plain. The revelation of this 'mystery' centers on the appearance of Jesus Christ in human history as the messianic King of kings."[2]

Read Ephesians 3:6.

4. In verse 6, Paul finally divulged the mystery. He used three compound nouns to make clear that both the Jewish believers and the Gentile believers were:

    a. Fellow _____

    b. Fellow _____ of the _____

    c. Fellow _____ of the _____ in Christ Jesus

The beautiful mystery of the love of God had been revealed to Paul. It was no longer just for the Jews but was also for the Gentiles—for all people. What a mystery it was! God became a man to do for us what we could not do for ourselves. In fact, there was no other way for our sin debt to be paid.

5. Paul wanted us to know that the gospel is for everyone, not just people like us. For Paul's readers it was a racial issue, but it goes beyond that. How do you feel about the fact that the gospel is for everyone—even terrorists, child molesters, and murderers?

FURTHER THOUGHTS:

DAY TWO

PAUL'S CALL TO THE GENTILES

Ephesians 3:7-13

HAVING FULLY DISCLOSED THE mystery of Christ in verses 2-6, Paul then shifted into an explanation of what compelled him to preach this mystery to the Gentiles.

> **Key Point:**
>
> We do all things through God's power.

Read Ephesians 3:7-13.

1. What gift initiated Paul's call to ministry? *(verse 7)*

2. What enabled him to continue his pursuit? *(verse 7)*

It was God's grace and the working of His power that made it possible for Paul to preach the gospel to the Gentiles. Again, nothing Paul did was by his own power. God made him a minister. He chose to use Paul, and Paul responded by doing whatever was necessary to carry out God's calling on his life.

3. What did Paul call himself? *(verse 8)*

It may sound a bit strange that Paul called himself "the very least of all saints," as he was widely known as a great preacher and missionary. At a first reading, it might not sound sincere. However, John Calvin vouched for Paul's humility in his commentary on Ephesians:

[Paul] is not speaking insincerely when he so lowers himself. Most men profess a feigned humility, while inwardly they swell with pride; in word they acknowledge themselves to be the least, while they wish to be regarded as supreme, and think themselves entitled to the highest honour. Paul is sincere in admitting his insignificance; indeed, he elsewhere speaks of himself far more meanly. 'For I am not worthy to be called an apostle' (1 Cor. 15:9). Again, when he calls himself the chief of sinners (1 Tim. 1:15).[3]

Paul consistently humbled himself in the pages of Scripture. This has a twofold effect. First, it makes clear to us that if even Paul was a sinful, unworthy person, then how much more are we? And second, it is once again a reminder that everything we do for God is through His power.

4. Paul divided his ministry into two specific functions. What were they? *(verses 8-9)*

   a.

   b.

5. Verse 8 uses the phrase "the unfathomable riches of Christ." What are some of those riches that you have received? (Feel free to take a look back at your "Benefits in Christ" chart on page 30.)

6. What was the purpose of Paul's ministry? *(verse 10)*

In Paul's day the division between Jews and Gentiles was the greatest division of all. With that in mind, unity among believers was a vast concern. It was big enough to send a huge message to "the rulers and the authorities in the heavenly places" (verse 10). It was proof that Jesus was truly in control of the universe.

7. Paul further explained that his ministry was a part of God's eternal design. How had God accomplished His eternal plan to unite the Jews and Gentiles into one body? *(verse 11)*

8. What did Paul say believers are granted through faith in Jesus Christ? *(verse 12)*

It cannot be said enough that our confidence does not come through us but through Christ. He provides the boldness we need.

9. Why did Paul think the believers might lose heart? *(verse 13)*

10. Paul had experienced severe tribulations in his life as a believer. **Read 1 Corinthians 4:9-13 and 2 Corinthians 11:24-29.** In what ways had Paul experienced suffering?

11. Why do you think Paul said his tribulations were for his readers' glory? *(verse 13)*

FURTHER THOUGHTS:

PAUL'S PRAYER FOR THE BELIEVERS

Ephesians 3:14-21

AT THIS POINT, PAUL resumed his prayer for the Ephesians. It was a prayer that was relevant not just to their lives but also to our own. As you read it, consider it to be a prayer for yourself.

Key Point:

We are God's beloved.

Read Ephesians 3:14-21.

1. What posture did Paul take as he began his prayer? *(verse 14)*

2. Do you use any certain postures when you pray? Why or why not? Do you think it makes a difference?

3. Paul praised the Fatherhood of God in verse 15. List some paternal characteristics of God.

> We must never forget that our inward man is the human spirit where God dwells, the place where the Spirit of the Lord is joined to our spirit. – Watchman Nee

4. What did Paul ask God to grant believers according to the riches of His glory? *(verse 16)*

The inner man refers to the innermost being of the believer. It is the part of man that is made alive in Christ. Watchman Nee said,

> We must never forget that our inward man is the human spirit where God dwells, the place where the Spirit of the Lord is joined to our spirit. Just as we are dressed in our clothing, so our inward man wears an outward man—i.e., our spirit wears our soul. Moreover the spirit and soul similarly wear the body. It is quite evident that men are generally more conscious of the outer man and the outermost man, but they hardly recognize their inner man, their spirit.[4]

5. Are you conscious of your "inner man"? Give some reasons why that might be important.

6. When Paul prayed that Christ would dwell in the hearts of believers, he was praying that Christ would be at home in their lives. As a result, what would happen in the lives of the believers? *(verse 17)*

7. Why did Paul pray that the believers would be rooted and grounded in love? *(verses 18-19)*

8. God's love is total. It is unrestrained and all-encompassing. No part of your life is beyond the majestic reach of His love. Record your thoughts about the love of God.

9. Paul closed this chapter with a doxology of praise to God in verses 20-21. What specifically did Paul reveal about the nature of God? *(verse 20)*

> Has the thunder of "God loved the world so much" been so muffled by the roar of religious rhetoric that we are deaf to the word that God could have tender feelings for us? Define yourself radically as one beloved by God. This is the true self. Every other identity is illusion. — BRENNAN MANNING

The word *glory* refers to the presence of Holy God. He alone deserves glory, honor, and praise. The ability to give God glory comes only through Jesus.

FURTHER THOUGHTS:

DAY FOUR

PRACTICAL APPLICATION

Ephesians 3

Key Point:

God's call is uncontainable!

READ EPHESIANS 3 AGAIN. What benefits of being in Christ did you discover as you read? Record them on your "Benefits in Christ" chart on page 30.

In Paul's day, there were people who were considered to be insiders (the Jews) and people who were considered to be outsiders (the Gentiles). Through Jesus Christ the barriers between the two were broken down. For the first time, the two groups heard through Paul's message that they were the same before God. The ground at the cross was level for all.

1. Fast-forward to today. Are there certain groups of people who are considered to be insiders and outsiders?

2. What are the barriers faced in and by the church today?

3. How can those walls be dismantled?

4. **Read James 2:1-7.** What does God say about partiality among believers?

When we realize the truth and breadth of the gospel message, we will not be able to contain God's call on our lives. Sharing His message with *all* people will be inevitable!

> It is not our church. It is God's church. Everyone is welcome in the house of God. — STEVE GAINES

FURTHER THOUGHTS:

SESSION 3 LISTENING GUIDE

UNCONTAINABLE!

Ephesians 3

By the word mystery we mean something known to the initiated, therefore if we are going to understand the gospel mystery of Sanctification and fully experience it, we must belong to the initiated, that is, we must be born from above by the Spirit of God.

— OSWALD CHAMBERS

1. **Equality in the Body** *(verses 1-12)*
   We understand the mystery.

   We have new power.

   We have new riches.

   We witness to the heavenly beings.

   We can be bold and confident (see Hebrews 4:14-16).

2. **The Family of God** *(verses 13-19)*
   God is the Creator of all mankind, but it is only as Savior that He is the Father of those who believe. There is no such thing as universalism. You must be born again in order to enter the kingdom of God.

   We have a God with a Father's heart (see John 1:12-14; 10:28-29; 1 John 3:1-3; John 17:23; Galatians 3:28–4:6; Hebrews 12:1-11; 1 Corinthians 13:4-8).

   We are rooted and grounded in love.

   We know who we are in Christ.

3. **The Super Abundance of Christ** *(verse 20)*
   The love of Christ and the power of Christ are beyond human expression or measure.

4. **To Him Be the Glory** *(verse 21)*
   When the church is faithful to God and steps out into an uncontainable ministry, God will be glorified!

WALK!

Ephesians 4:1-16

In light of all this, here's what I want you to do. While I'm locked up here, a prisoner for the Master, I want you to get out there and walk—better yet, run!—on the road God called you to travel. I don't want any of you sitting around on your hands. I don't want anyone strolling off, down some path that goes nowhere. And mark that you do this with humility and discipline—not in fits and starts, but steadily, pouring yourselves out for each other in acts of love, alert at noticing differences and quick at mending fences.

—EPHESIANS 4:1-3 (MSG)

THE EPISTLE OF EPHESIANS has two major divisions. Chapters 1–3 are doctrinal in emphasis, while chapters 4–6 are practical. Throughout the remainder of this letter, Paul exhorted the Ephesians to live mature lives in unity with each other. The early church faced many challenges. Paul encouraged the first-century church to embrace their diversity while maintaining unity. This truth is just as applicable today as it was twenty centuries ago. If the church is to rise to its true stature in accomplishing the purposes of God, then its members must recognize their own unique giftedness in Christ and "walk—better yet, run" (Ephesians 4:1, MSG) in a way that brings honor to Him.

Day 1: One Body *(Ephesians 4:1-6)*
We are to walk in unity.

Day 2: The Gifts of the Body *(Ephesians 4:7-13)*
We are to use our gifts for God's glory.

Day 3: A Mature Body *(Ephesians 4:13-16)*
We are to mature in our faith.

Day 4: Practical Application *(Ephesians 4:1-16)*
We must walk worthily!

DAY ONE

ONE BODY

Ephesians 4:1-6

The Christian church cannot rise to its true stature in accomplishing the purposes of God when its members operate largely through the gifts of nature, neglecting the true gifts and graces of the spirit of God.

—A. W. TOZER

IN CHAPTER 4, PAUL continued the theme of unity. He added to his proclamation that the church is to be united and explained how we are to live as the body of Christ.

> **Key Point:**
>
> We are to walk in unity.

Read Ephesians 4:1-3.

1. With what exhortation did Paul open chapter 4? *(verse 1)*

The Greek word for *worthy* is *axios*. The word implies that believers are to keep their lives and their calling equally in balance as if they were on a set of scales. Simply said, our actions should reflect our spiritual calling.

> We cannot expect the world to believe that the Father sent the Son, that Jesus' claims are true and that Christianity is true, unless the world sees some reality of the oneness of true Christians. – FRANCIS SCHAEFFER

2. Paul listed four characteristics that are present in the lives of those who are walking in a manner worthy of their calling. What are they? How do you define each trait? *(verse 2)*

a.

b.

c.

d.

Humility is an attitude; gentleness is the result of having humility. Similarly, patience is an attitude and "showing tolerance for one another in love" (verse 2) is the outcome.

3. What are some examples of times when we need to patiently bear with one another in love?

4. Humility, gentleness, patience, and bearing with one another will produce a spirit of unity among believers. What bond did Paul say would unite those who follow Christ? *(verse 3)*

5. Who do you strive to emulate spiritually?

While it's good to look to mature Christians to see how to live, the best place to look is at Jesus. Read what A. W. Tozer had to say about this:

Has it ever occurred to you that one hundred pianos all tuned to the same fork are automatically tuned to each other? They are of one accord by being tuned, not to each other, but to another standard to which each one must individually bow. So one hundred worshippers met together, each one looking away to Christ, are in heart nearer to each other than they could possibly be were they to become "unity" conscious and turn their eyes away from God to strive for closer fellowship. Social religion is perfected when private religion is purified. The body becomes stronger as its members become healthier. The whole church of God gains when the members that compose it begin to seek a better and higher life.[1]

Read Ephesians 4:4-6. Peter Meiderlin, a theologian and pastor living in Augsburg during the early seventeenth century, penned these words: *"In necessariis unitas, in non-necessariis libertas, in utrisque caritas."* Translated, this says, "In the essentials unity, in the nonessentials liberty, in all things charity." Paul understood that there would be some nonessential differences among believers. However, in verses 4-6 he listed seven essential "ones" upon which the Holy Spirit builds unity.

6. What are the seven essentials? *(verses 4-6)*

a.

b.

c.

d.

e.

f.

g.

7. What do we learn about God? *(verse 6)*

We have *one* God (in three persons), and He rules over and in everything. What an assuring truth!

FURTHER THOUGHTS:

DAY TWO

THE GIFTS OF THE BODY

Ephesians 4:7-13

IN VERSES 1-6, PAUL wrote about unity within the body of Christ. With verse 7, he began to discuss the individuals who make up that body.

Key Point:

We are to use our gifts for God's glory.

Read Ephesians 4:7-10.

1. What has every believer been given? *(verse 7)*

2. The grace bestowed upon believers refers to the spiritual gifts Christ gave to them. Paul listed the spiritual gifts in Ephesians 4:11; Romans 12:3-8; 1 Corinthians 12; and 1 Peter 4:10-11. As you read through these lists, which gift(s) do you see evidence of in your life?

Many questions often swirl around the discussion of spiritual gifts. Let's look to *The Reformation Study Bible* for some answers:

Amid many debated questions regarding spiritual gifts in the New Testament, three certainties stand out. First, a spiritual gift is an ability to express, celebrate, display, and so communicate Christ in a way that builds up and strengthens the faith of other Christians and enlarges the church. Second, spiritual gifts may be broadly classified as either abilities of speech or of loving, practical helpfulness. In Rom. 12:6-8, Paul's list of gifts alternates between the categories: prophecy, teaching, and exhorting are gifts of speech; serving, giving, leading, and showing mercy are gifts of helpfulness. However much they differ as forms of human activity, all are of equal dignity when one properly uses the gift one has (1 Pet. 4:10, 11). Third, no Christian is without some gift of ministry (1 Cor. 12:7; Eph. 4:7). It is every believer's responsibility to find, develop, and fully use whatever capacities for service God has given.[2]

> As each one has received a special gift, employ it in serving one another as good stewards of the manifold grace of God. – 1 Peter 4:10

Regardless of how we may think or feel at a certain time about our gifts, we can rest assured that we have at least one and that each gift is just as important as any other when used in the way God wants us to use it to serve others and glorify Him. There is no "gift hierarchy."

Read Ephesians 4:8-9 again. In these verses, Paul was referring to what the psalmist wrote in Psalm 68:18: "You have ascended on high, You have led captive Your captives; You have received gifts among men, even among the rebellious also, that the LORD God may dwell there." The picture being painted in both passages was of a military conqueror leading captives to victory and then giving gifts to his followers.

3. In light of the victory Christ won at the cross, how are you using your gift(s) to glorify the one who gave His life for you?

Read Ephesians 4:11-12.

4. Paul wrote that some gifts were given to people to use specifically in church leadership roles. What positions did Paul list? *(verse 11)*

5. All of these specially gifted people had one purpose. What was it? *(verse 12)*

6. **Read 1 Corinthians 12:12-20.** Summarize Paul's message.

7. How did God speak to you through the 1 Corinthians 12 passage?

FURTHER THOUGHTS:

A MATURE BODY

Ephesians 4:13-16

Key Point:

We are to mature in our faith.

IN THESE VERSES, PAUL expanded again on the idea of unity. As a unified church, we are to manifest the characteristics and qualities of Christ.

Read Ephesians 4:13-16.

1. Describe a mature Christian. *(verses 13,15)*

2. Describe someone who is immature in his or her faith. *(verse 14)*

It is important to study God's Word and grow in His truth and as imitators of Christ so we may become mature believers. Why? Take a look at what the *Women's Evangelical Commentary* has to say:

> Growing in the knowledge of Christ provides protection from confusion over false doctrine. Knowing the truths of God is arguably one of the best defenses against the enemy, who clearly has many "techniques of deceit." Growth in Christ is accomplished by speaking the truth in love, which means sitting under preaching and leadership that is truthful according to Scripture (Eph. 4:15). It also means living in an authentic Christian way, which should protect individuals and the church from evil and deception.[3]

We see that maturity means not only know-ing the truth but also speaking it. And we don't just speak the truth; we speak it "in love." In addition, we are to live authentically. There is obviously much to the maturity process. As Ephesians 4:15 says, "We are to grow up in *all aspects* into Him who is the head," that is, Jesus (emphasis added). There is not just one thing that will make us mature Christians. It is a process, but it is a necessary one.

> God wants us to grow up, to know the whole truth and tell it in love – like Christ in everything. We take our lead from Christ, who is the source of everything we do.
> — EPHESIANS 4:15 (MSG)

3. Describe your own faith. Where does it fall on a scale from immature to mature? In what ways do you need to become more mature?

FURTHER THOUGHTS:

DAY FOUR

PRACTICAL APPLICATION

Ephesians 4:1-16

Key Point:

We must walk worthily!

READ EPHESIANS 4:1-16 AGAIN. As you read through it, add items to your "Benefits in Christ" chart on page 30.

1. Which of the verses in this week's passage speaks to you the most? Why?

2. In what specific ways might you better use your spiritual gifts to bring glory to God?

3. In what ways might you need to change your attitudes, words, or actions in order to walk in a manner that is worthy of God's calling?

> *Our Lord's making of a disciple is supernatural. He does not build on any natural capacity at all. God does not ask us to do the things that are easy to us naturally. He only asks us to do the things we are perfectly fitted to do by His grace, and the cross will come along that line always.*[4]

> —OSWALD CHAMBERS

FURTHER THOUGHTS:

WALK!

Ephesians 4:1-16

We sit forever with Christ, that we may walk continuously before men.

—WATCHMAN NEE, *SIT, WALK, STAND*

1. **Walk Worthily** *(verses 1-2)*
   Humility *(tapeinophrosune)*—lowliness of mind, humble-minded[5]

   Gentleness *(prautes)*—consideration, meekness

   Patience *(makrothumia)*—patience in respect to persons

   Forbearance *(anechomai)*—to hold up against a thing, to bear with, endure

   Love *(agape)*—benevolent love

2. **Diligently Preserve Unity** *(verses 3-6)*
   Diligence *(spoudazo)*—to give diligence, make every effort

   Peace *(eirene)*—rest in contrast with strife; denoting the absence or end of strife

3. **Use Your Gifts** *(verses 7-12)*
   The gifts of the Spirit: 1 Corinthians 12:4-11,14-18,27-31; Romans
   12:3-21; Ephesians 4:11

   - Apostle
   - Prophet
   - Teacher
   - Pastor
   - Working of Miracles
   - Discernment of Spirits
   - Word of Wisdom, Knowledge
   - Evangelist
   - Encourager/Exhorter
   - Faith
   - Healing
   - Speaking in Tongues
   - Interpretation of Tongues
   - Ministry/Serving
   - Administration
   - Leadership
   - Helps
   - Mercy
   - Giving

4. **Grow Up** *(verses 13-16)*
   We must aspire to attain to the fullness of Christ so that when
   people are in our presence, they see Jesus Christ.

   We must always speak the truth in love.

   We must cooperate with one another.

CHANGED!

Ephesians 4:17-32

Everything—and I do mean everything—connected with that old way of life has to go. It's rotten through and through. Get rid of it! And then take on an entirely new way of life—a God-fashioned life, a life renewed from the inside and working itself into your conduct as God accurately reproduces his character in you.

—EPHESIANS 4:22-24 (MSG)

THERE SHOULD BE A noticeable difference between the life of the believer and the life of the unbeliever. All evidence of the old life must be eradicated. No more excuses. No more secret sins. A changed life is one that has been *transformed* from the old life, *reformed* into a new life, and *conformed* to the character of Christ. That is the "God-fashioned" life. In his book *Celebration of Discipline*, Richard Foster wrote, "As we travel this path, the blessing of God will come upon us and reconstruct us into the image of Jesus. We must remember that the path does not produce the change; it only places us where the change can occur."[1] Lord, keep us in that place where we can be changed from the inside out!

Day 1: A Warning *(Ephesians 4:17-19)*
Don't live like an unbeliever.

Day 2: An Admonition *(Ephesians 4:20-24)*
Live a holy and righteous new life.

Day 3: A Challenge *(Ephesians 4:25-32)*
Put away sin.

Day 4: Practical Application *(Ephesians 4:17-32)*
We are changed!

DAY ONE

A WARNING

Ephesians 4:17-19

No one enters into the experience of entire sanctification without going through a "white funeral"—the burial of the old life. . . . Have you had your "white funeral," or are you sacredly playing the fool with your soul? Is there a place in your life marked as the last day, a place to which the memory goes back with a chastened and extraordinary grateful remembrance—yes, it was then, at that "white funeral" that I made an agreement with God.

—OSWALD CHAMBERS

Key Point:

Don't live like an unbeliever.

IN THE FIRST HALF of chapter 4, Paul spoke at length about unity among believers. In verse 17 it may seem at first like he changed the topic as he warned against living like unbelievers. However, is this not a continuation of the theme of unity? The believers in Ephesus were surrounded by wickedness and immorality, and their unity as a church would undoubtedly help them shun the sinful life and move toward Christlikeness.

Read Ephesians 4:17-19. In these three short verses, Paul revealed a number of characteristics of the surrounding unbelieving Gentiles that he did not want the Ephesians to emulate.

1. Make a list of the words Paul used to describe the Gentiles' way of life. *(verses 17-19)*

The words "impurity with greediness" (verse 19) paint the picture of someone who is in a constant state of self-gratification, lusting after every form of impurity, always wanting more, never satisfied.

Read Romans 1:18-32.

2. What is God's response to those who are greedy in their impurity? *(Romans 1:24,26,28)*

> And so I insist — and God backs me up on this — that there be no going along with the crowd, the empty-headed, mindless crowd. They've refused for so long to deal with God that they've lost touch not only with God but with reality itself. They can't think straight anymore. Feeling no pain, they let themselves go in sexual obsession, addicted to every sort of perversion. — EPHESIANS 4:17-19 (MSG)

3. What are the results of living a life driven by a lust for impurity? *(Romans 1:29-32)*

When someone becomes focused on living a sinful life and doing impure things, God will let her do it. Even more tragically, those impure actions will lead to even more unrighteousness, to the point that while she knows what God says about sin, she fully approves of it.

4. Does any of that sound familiar? How does what you have learned about the culture of Ephesus compare to our own culture?

There is a difference between those who know they're in a sinful state and want to get out and those who don't. Consider the words of John Ensor:

> Sheep and swine can both end up in the mire. Yet the essential difference in their two natures is quite visible from the reaction each has to its fallen condition. While sheep do stray and stumble into the mire, they quickly loathe the situation and struggle to get free. They may be dirty, but they desire to be clean. They may be

stuck, but they bleat for their shepherd to come and save them out of the muck. But swine, in keeping with their nature, wallow in the muck, content to stay there all day.[2]

FURTHER THOUGHTS:

DAY TWO

AN ADMONITION

Ephesians 4:20-24

AFTER WARNING THE EPHESIAN believers not to live as the Gentiles do, Paul reminded them of the new life they had in Christ. They didn't have to live like unbelievers. Instead they were to reject that old life and take hold of a new one.

| **Key Point:** |
| Live a holy and righteous new life. |

Read Ephesians 4:20-24.

1. In Ephesians 4:17-19, Paul used the word *they* to refer to the unbelieving Gentiles. What made the difference for the believers Paul was addressing in his letter? *(verse 20)*

2. It was Christ that made the difference. In what ways has Jesus made a difference in your life?

3. What did Paul say was "in Jesus"? *(verse 21)*

In his New Testament commentary, John MacArthur said, "The truth about salvation leads to the fullness of truth about God, man, creation, history, life, purpose, relationships, heaven, hell, judgment, and

Are you content to maintain a "certain level of sin" in your life, as long as you can tame and manage it? Mark it down: There is no such thing as a small sin. Every unconfessed sin is a seed that will produce a multiplied harvest. — NANCY LEIGH DEMOSS

everything else that is truly important."[3] The truth we find in Jesus leads us to all other truth.

4. What instruction did Paul give regarding the old self? *(verse 22)*

It's not always easy to put off the old self, but it is vitally necessary that we get rid of it completely. Nancy Leigh DeMoss addressed this in her book *Holiness*:

> Are you content to maintain a "certain level of sin" in your life, as long as you can tame and manage it? Mark it down: There is no such thing as a small sin. Every unconfessed sin is a seed that will produce a multiplied harvest. As Charles Spurgeon warned, "Those who tolerate sin in what they think to be little things will soon indulge it in greater matters."[4]

5. After Paul told the Ephesians to "lay aside" the old self, he gave two instructions regarding their new life in Christ. What were his instructions? *(verses 23-24)*

a.

b.

6. How did Paul define the new self? *(verse 24)*

This new self is a transformation of the old self that gave itself over to impurities. It is not just a change of character. The old self is gone, and the new has come, created in the likeness of God, reflecting God's righteousness and holiness.

FURTHER THOUGHTS:

DAY THREE

A CHALLENGE

Ephesians 4:25-32

Key Point:

Put away sin.

AFTER ADMONISHING THE EPHESIANS to lay aside the old self and put on the new, Paul told them several specific ways to do just that. He listed ways to live righteously with the help of God's Spirit, and he warned against getting caught up in certain sins.

Read Ephesians 4:25-32.

1. In these verses, Paul juxtaposed "old self" behaviors with "new self" behaviors. As you read these verses again, list the opposing behaviors in the space given.

Old Self	New Self

2. Satan can use anger to destroy unity and love among believers. What did Paul say the Devil could gain through anger? *(verse 27)*

Ephesians 4:27 tells us that the Enemy is looking for an opportunity to gain a foothold in our lives to work his ruin. We give the Enemy "an opportunity" when we allow him to exercise influence over us by the sin in our lives. That is not to say that every time we sin we give the Devil a foothold in our lives. We give him rights into our lives when we refuse to let go of our sin, confess it, and turn completely from it.

> However holy or Christlike a Christian may become, he is still in the condition of "being changed."
> — *Life Application Bible Commentary*

Francis Frangipane has some advice about dealing with the Devil in this situation: "A vital key, therefore, to overcoming the devil is humility. To humble yourself is to refuse to defend your image: you *are* corrupt and full of sin in your old nature! Yet, we have a *new* nature which has been created in the likeness of Christ (Eph. 4:24), so we can agree with our adversary about the condition of our flesh."[5]

3. How do believers grieve the Holy Spirit? *(verse 30)*

We grieve God's Spirit when we rebel against Him and refuse to grab hold of His righteousness in the new life He has offered us in exchange for our old life of sin. It is in choosing sin over righteousness—in whatever form that takes—that we grieve Him. This also relates back to the theme of unity discussed earlier in chapter 4. When we sin, we disrupt the unity of believers, and subsequently we grieve the Holy Spirit.

> To be a Christian means to forgive the inexcusable, because God has forgiven the inexcusable in you.
> — C. S. Lewis

Paul finished his challenge to righteous living in verses 31-32 by summarizing what a holy life doesn't look like and what it does look like. And finally, at the end of verse 32, he reminded the Ephesians of the reason for their salvation.

4. By what standard did Paul say we should forgive each other? *(verse 32)*

If we compare the sins we have committed against God to those other people have committed against us, we have no reason to not forgive others as God forgave us. Because of our sins, the only sinless man—God's Son—had to die. If God can forgive us for that, surely we can forgive others for the things they have done against us.

FURTHER THOUGHTS:

DAY FOUR

PRACTICAL APPLICATION

Ephesians 4:17-32

Read Ephesians 4:17-32 again.

1. Have you laid aside the old self and put on the new? If not, why? What might you need to do in order to put on the new self?

Key Point:
We are changed!

2. What types of communication would you label as unwholesome or corrupt? *(verse 29)*

3. What are some examples of words that build up or edify?

4. On a scale of 1 (holding grudges) to 10 (easily forgiving), how would you rate yourself as a forgiving person?

5. Have you ever withheld forgiveness from someone? If so, what was your reason for doing so? What happened in the end?

6. Is there someone you need to extend forgiveness to now? What holds you back? How can you overcome the obstacles to forgiveness?

Forgiveness is God's invention for coming to terms with a world in which, despite their best intentions, people are unfair to each other and hurt each other deeply. He began by forgiving us. And he invites us all to forgive each other. — Lewis B. Smedes

FURTHER THOUGHTS:

SESSION 5 LISTENING GUIDE

CHANGED!

Ephesians 4:17-32

The renewal of the mind in salvation brings not simply a renovation of character, but transformation of the old self to the new self.
— JOHN MACARTHUR

1. **Tragic Reminder** *(verses 17-19)*
   Don't have a hard heart.
   Don't become desensitized to sin.

2. **Take Off the Old** *(verses 20-22)*
   Warning signs that we're slipping into the flesh:

   • Yellow

   • Red

   Who will you allow to define your reality — God and His Word or
   the world and the Enemy, who is at work around us?

3. **Put On the New** *(verses 23-25,32)*
   We are renewed in the spirit of our minds.
   We are created in:

   • Righteousness
   • Holiness
   • Truth

We are to be:

- Kind
- Tenderhearted
- Forgiving

4. **Don't Open the Door to the Enemy** *(verses 26-28)*
    Don't give the Devil ground in your life.
    Don't allow anger to stay in your life unchecked.
    Strongholds of the Enemy: pride, fear, anger, lust, unforgiveness,
        lying, stealing, unbelief, greed

    Strongholds are wrong ways of thinking that must be dealt with
        through repentance and confession. We must take back the
        ground we have given to the Enemy and replace the lies with the
        truth of God's Word.

5. **Watch Your Mouth** *(verse 29)*
    Proverbs 18:20-21
    Matthew 12:34
    Proverbs 23:7

6. **Do Not Grieve the Holy Spirit** *(verses 30-32)*
    We have the Spirit within us and we can sense His presence.

    We cannot tolerate any sin in our lives.

IMITATE!

Ephesians 5:1-21

Watch what God does, and then you do it, like children who learn proper behavior from their parents. Mostly what God does is love you. Keep company with him and learn a life of love. Observe how Christ loved us. His love was not cautious but extravagant. He didn't love in order to get something from us but to give everything of himself to us. Love like that.

—EPHESIANS 5:1-2 (MSG)

IF YOU HAVE CHILDREN, you probably remember them imitating you. My girls loved to play "dress up" and pretend they were either getting married or were married with children. One of my favorite gifts is one our oldest daughter, Lindsey, gave me at her bridesmaid luncheon. The gift was a frame with two slots. One had a picture of her dressed in a wedding dress costume at age three. The other side had this verse on it: "Train a child in the way he should go, and when he is old he will not turn from it" (Proverbs 22:6, NIV). Under the verse was written, "Insert wedding photo." As you can well imagine, the tears began to flow when I opened this gift. How had the little girl who imitated grown-ups become one? As God's children, we are to imitate Him until we become like Him, when we see Him face-to-face.

Day 1: A Mandate to Imitate *(Ephesians 5:1-2)*
We are to imitate God.

Day 2: A Model of Light *(Ephesians 5:3-14)*
We are to walk in the light.

Day 3: A Case for Wisdom *(Ephesians 5:15-21)*
We are to be filled with the Spirit.

Day 4: Practical Application *(Ephesians 5:1-21)*
We are to imitate Christ!

DAY ONE

A MANDATE TO IMITATE

Ephesians 5:1-2

God does not give us power to love as He loves; the love of God, the very nature of God, possesses us, and He loves through us.

—OSWALD CHAMBERS

IN CHAPTER 4, PAUL told the Ephesians to not live like the unbelieving Gentiles, but instead to put on the new life they had in Christ. He gave specific instructions about how they were to live and were not to live. The theme of righteous living is continued here in chapter 5.

Key Point:

We are to imitate God.

Read Ephesians 5:1-2.

1. What is our mandate? *(verses 1-2)*

Verse 1 begins with, "Therefore," which refers back to verse 32 of chapter 4. We imitate God and walk in love because we have received His love and forgiveness—because we have put off the old self and taken on the new. *The New International Commentary on the New Testament* says, "Some of the divine attributes lie far beyond our scope even to measure, much more to copy; but there are communicable perfections which present to us a glorious field of emulation; and forgiving love is conspicuous among these approximately imitable traits of Deity."[1]

We should not take the mandate to imitate God lightly. It is the main thing we should strive for as Christians. John MacArthur said:

The Christian has no greater calling or purpose than imitating his Lord. That is the very purpose of sanctification, growing in likeness to the Lord while serving Him on earth (cf. Matt. 5:48). The Christian life is designed to reproduce godliness as modeled by the Savior and Lord, Jesus Christ, in whose image believers have been recreated through the New Birth. . . . As God's dear children, believers are to become more and more like their heavenly Father.[2]

> The Christian has no greater calling or purpose than imitating his Lord. That is the very purpose of sanctification, growing in likeness to the Lord while serving Him on earth.
> — JOHN MACARTHUR

In verses 1-2 Paul reminds us of three things about God. First, we are His children, which means that He is our Father. Second, Christ is our Savior who gave up His own life as a sacrifice for us. And finally, He loves us. As image-bearers of God, we are to imitate Him as a way of showing the world who He is — Father, Savior, and love.

2. **Read Mark 12:28-31.** What is the greatest commandment?

3. **Read John 15:12-17.** Who are we to love?

4. **Read John 13:34-35.** How will others know that we are Christ's disciples?

In 1 John 4:8 the Lord says, "The one who does not love does not know God, for God is love." If we know and love the Lord — who is Himself love — we will also love one another.

5. **Read Isaiah 58:6-12.** List the aspects of the fast that God desires.

6. In Isaiah 58, what does God say He will do if we honor Him by serving others?

God does not desire for us to merely perform religious rituals but to love as He loves and to serve as Christ served.

7. **Read Matthew 20:24-28.** What did Jesus say He came to do?

In *The New International Commentary on the New Testament* we read, "We have all the power we need to live this life of divine love. Christ has given us His very Spirit. This Christ, who is both 'offering and sacrifice'—as John Wessel, one of the precursors of the Reformation, reminds us—is Priest and Victim in one."[3]

Christ has secured our forgiveness that we might freely offer it to others. We are to walk in love as imitators of Christ.

FURTHER THOUGHTS:

DAY TWO

A MODEL OF LIGHT

Ephesians 5:3-14

Key Point:

We are to walk in the light.

THE LINES HAVE BEEN drawn, and it is very clear that a Christian's conduct should reflect Christ. Ephesus was a city much like the cities and nation in which we live. Materialism, spiritualism, immorality, and greed were rampant. We are not to look like the world but to imitate God in action and speech.

Read Ephesians 5:3-14.

1. What three things did Paul forbid? *(verse 3)*

2. How did Paul describe the speech that we are to avoid? *(verse 4)*

The sins of the tongue are actually sins of the heart, as we learn in Matthew 15:18: "But the things that proceed out of the mouth come from the heart, and those defile the man." Our speech should reflect a heart that has been changed and is full of thanksgiving and gratitude for all we have in Christ.

3. What should we not allow to deceive us? *(verse 6)*

4. We read that we are to walk as children of what? *(verse 8)*

Jesus said in John 8:12, "I am the Light of the world; he who follows Me will not walk in the darkness, but will have the Light of life." When we walk with Jesus, He will light our way and we will be able to clearly see what is good and true and righteous.

5. We are to learn what is pleasing to the Lord. How are you pleasing God? *(verse 10)*

> You groped your way through that murk once, but no longer. You're out in the open now. The bright light of Christ makes your way plain. So no more stumbling around. Get on with it! The good, the right, the true — these are the actions appropriate for daylight hours. Figure out what will please Christ, and then do it. — Ephesians 5:8-10 (msg)

6. We are not to participate in the deeds of darkness but instead to do what? *(verses 11-12)*

We cannot live both in the light and in the darkness. We must choose one or the other, and as imitators of God, we must choose the light. As for the deeds of darkness, we are commanded to "have nothing to do with [them]" (verse 11, NIV).

7. Once the light exposes dark deeds, we are to rid ourselves of them (verses 13-14). Has God revealed something to you during this study that you have had to repent of and get rid of?

FURTHER THOUGHTS:

DAY THREE

A CASE FOR WISDOM

Ephesians 5:15-21

Key Point:

We are to be filled with the Spirit.

Read Ephesians 5:15-17.

1. How are we to walk? What will that walk look like? *(verse 15)*

What does it mean to live wisely? In a nutshell, we are to live like Jesus. We are to walk in His light and imitate His actions. How do we know what it looks like to imitate Jesus? We read about Him in the Gospels and see how He conducted Himself in all kinds of situations. We read about His character in Paul's letters. And we seek to imitate Him in all that we do.

2. Why are we to make the most of our time? *(verse 16)*

In the *Women's Evangelical Commentary*, we read, "This section is a wakeup call. Do not be consumed with the world and the demands of everyday life, but realize what this life means in the greater perspective of eternity. . . . Realize that life on earth is brief and should not be wasted."[4] We have only a short time here on earth, and our purpose is to be image-bearers of Christ—to show the world who He is.

Verse 17 tells us not to be foolish, but instead to understand the will of the Lord.

Do not be consumed with the world and the demands of everyday life, but realize what this life means in the greater perspective of eternity.

— *WOMEN'S EVANGELICAL COMMENTARY*

---

3. **Read Romans 12:1-2.** How do we discern the will of the Lord?

4. Are you able to discern the will of the Lord? If not, what do you think might be keeping you from it?

Read Ephesians 5:18-21.

5. What two states of being did Paul contrast? *(verse 18)*

It may seem a bit odd to read about drunkenness here. However, think back to Acts 2, on the day of Pentecost, when the disciples were filled with the Spirit and accused of being drunk. We all know that the words and actions of an intoxicated person are greatly influenced by the alcohol, and the observers in Acts 2 thought the odd actions of the disciples were brought on by intoxication, when in fact they weren't. Paul was saying in his letter to the Ephesians that we should be influenced and filled not by wine but by the Spirit of God. It should be evident in how we walk and talk to the extent that our hearts overflow in praise, singing, and thanking God for all things, and that we choose to subject ourselves to one another in the fear of Christ.

Warren Wiersbe said, "'Be filled with the Spirit' is God's command, and He expects us to obey. The command is plural, so it applies to all Christians and not just to a select few. The verb is in the present tense — 'to keep being filled' — so it is an experience we should enjoy constantly and not just on special occasions."[5]

6. How are we to speak to one another? *(verse 19)*

7. What are we to give thanks for? *(verse 20)*

8. What are we told to do? *(verse 21)*

To be "subject to one another" means that we put the other's needs and desires above our own. Romans 12:9-10 says it this way: "Let love be without hypocrisy. Abhor what is evil; cling to what is good. Be devoted to one another in brotherly love; give preference to one another in honor."

Being filled with the Spirit will enable us to live the life of love that Christ commanded. The fruits of the Spirit are listed for us in Galatians 5:22-23: love, joy, peace, patience, kindness, goodness, faithfulness, gentleness, and self-control. What a beautiful and fragrant life!

FURTHER THOUGHTS:

DAY FOUR

PRACTICAL APPLICATION

Ephesians 5:1-21

Read Ephesians 5:1-21 again.

1. When we imitate God and please Him, what will our lives look like?

Key Point:

We are to imitate Christ!

2. Does your life look like the kind of life God would commend and one that proves you are Christ's disciple?

3. What adjustments do you need to make to more closely imitate God?

FURTHER THOUGHTS:

IMITATE!

Ephesians 5:1-21

*"He who follows me does not walk in darkness," says the Lord. These
are the words of Christ by which we are advised to imitate his life
and ways, if we desire truly to be enlightened and to be freed from
all blindness of the heart. Let it therefore be our chief preoccupation
to think upon the life of Jesus Christ.*

—Thomas à Kempis

1. **Imitate God** *(verse 1)*
   Lessons from storms (Matthew 8:23-27; Mark 6:45-52)

   In what ways are we to imitate God?
   Matthew 5:48; Luke 6:36; Ephesians 4:32

2. **Walk in Love** *(verses 2-9)*
   Isaiah 58

   • What are the religious rituals?

- What is the fast that God has chosen?

- What are the blessings that God promises?

3. **Walk in a Manner Pleasing to the Lord** *(verses 10-17)*
   Romans 12:2
   Matthew 25:14-30 (the parable of the talents)
   Luke 12:22-34

Ledger of Eternal Investments

Time	Money

2 Corinthians 9:8

4. **Be Filled with the Spirit** *(verses 18-21)*
   Evidences of the Spirit

Examine yourself (2 Corinthians 13:5)

REFLECT!

Ephesians 5:22–6:9

Wives, be subject to your own husbands, as to the Lord.
— EPHESIANS 5:22

THE FIRST PART OF Ephesians 5 calls us to imitate God and to love as He loves us. Then in Ephesians 5:18 we are commanded to be filled with His Spirit. It is only through the filling of God's Holy Spirit that our relationships can reflect Christ and bring Him glory. Are your relationships causing you to become more like Christ? How can we be sure this is happening in our marriage, with our children, and in the workplace?

Day 1: A Directive for Wives *(Ephesians 5:22-24)*
Wives should respect their husbands.

Day 2: A Directive for Husbands *(Ephesians 5:25-33)*
Husbands should love their wives.

Day 3: A Directive for Family and Workplace Relationships *(Ephesians 6:1-9)*
Everyone should submit to authority.

Day 4: Practical Application *(Ephesians 5:22–6:9)*
Our relationships should reflect Christ!

DAY ONE

A DIRECTIVE FOR WIVES

Ephesians 5:22-24

A wedding calls us to our highest and best—in fact, to almost impossible—ideals. It's the way we want to live. But marriage reminds us of the daily reality of living as sinful human beings in a radically broken world.

—GARY THOMAS

Key Point:

Wives should respect their husbands.

IN THE LAST PART of Ephesians 5, Paul focused on the foundational relationship of marriage. Marriage was the first institution that God ordained. It was for this reason that Adam was commanded to leave his father and mother and cleave to his wife, that the two might become one. This relationship is the backbone of civilization, and it was the means by which God would not only populate the world but also train men and women to represent Him. And yet it is in this relationship that our Christianity is put to the test.

Read Ephesians 5:22-31.

1. What did Paul tell wives they are to do? *(verse 22)*

2. What emotions do you experience when you hear the word *submit*?

The Greek word translated "submit" or "be subject to" is *hupotasso*, which means to "place in an orderly fashion under."[1] God is a God of order, and we are to follow His order for the home to be harmonious.

Headship is not dictatorship; instead, it is each for the other and both for the Lord. The *Bible Reader's Companion* says:

> To make sure that we do not misunderstand headship in marriage as the right of a husband to dominate his wife, Paul specifies in which way the husband's headship is to be expressed. Specifically the husband is the head, "as Christ loved the church and gave Himself for her, to make her holy" (vv. 25-26). In marriage headship emphasizes the husband's Christlike role of sustaining and protecting his wife and encouraging her personal and spiritual growth.[2]

Take a look, also, at what John MacArthur had to say about the issue of submission:

> Remember, Paul's theme in Ephesians 5 (from verse 21) is mutual submission. When he introduced the husband's headship in verse 23, he was not changing the subject. He was not saying everyone else needs to submit to the man, who as the head of the family gets to impose his will and his desires on everyone else. Not at all. Paul's whole point here was that a husband best shows Christlike headship by voluntary, loving sacrifice and service on behalf of the wife—which is as much a form of submission as the wife's allegiance to her husband's leadership and the children's obedience to their parents.[3]

3. What if, as author Gary Thomas suggested, "God designed marriage to make us holy more than to make us happy"?[4] How does your marriage bring out areas of your flesh that God is exposing for you to become more like Christ? What specific area have you been aware of recently?

In marriage headship emphasizes the husband's Christlike role of sustaining and protecting his wife and encouraging her personal and spiritual growth. — *Bible Reader's Companion*

> God designed marriage to make us holy more than to make us happy. — GARY THOMAS

4. Verses 23-24 compare our relationship to our husbands with the relationship of the church to Christ. How do these verses tell us to relate to our husbands?

Read Philippians 2:1-11.

5. We are to be imitators of Christ. How will you follow His example?

We are not to live in competition with our husbands but in cooperation with them. There is a mutual love and respect that is to be exhibited in the home as we live and love like Christ. In the context in which the book of Ephesians was written, God was actually increasing the value of women and elevating them to equality with their husbands in Christ. Yet *The Teacher's Commentary* makes it very clear that He has given us different roles in the home:

> What a contrast with the pagan view! Suddenly things are reversed. The wife is transformed from an unimportant adjunct, who exists only to meet her husband's needs, to a person of intrinsic worth and value, becoming the focus of her husband's concern. Instead of demanding that she live for him, he begins to live for her! Rather than keeping her under, he seeks to lift her up. Christian headship lifts the wife up as the rightful object of a husband's loving concern. In this context, the husband serves by being a Christlike head; the wife serves in responsive submission to one who lifts her up and holds her beside him.[5]

6. There are parallel passages in the New Testament that teach these same relationship principles. **Read and compare Ephesians 5:22, Colossians 3:18, and 1 Peter 3:1.** What does each passage command?

a. Ephesians 5:22

b. Colossians 3:18

c. 1 Peter 3:1

Notice that in 1 Peter 3:1 great emphasis is given to the wife's behavior. Unbelieving or disobedient husbands can actually be won to the Lord without a word from their wives. They are won by their behavior. Is it obvious by your submission and respect for your husband that you have a vital and intimate relationship with Christ?

FURTHER THOUGHTS:

DAY TWO

A DIRECTIVE FOR HUSBANDS

Ephesians 5:25-33

Key Point:

Husbands should love their wives.

SOME PEOPLE READ THE verses about wives submitting to their husbands and then stop reading. However, there is a flip side to the equation. It would be disastrous for a husband to expect his wife to submit to him if he were not also taking on the role and expectations God has for him.

Read Ephesians 5:25-33.

1. Husbands are commanded to love like Christ. Describe that love. *(verse 25)*

2. What will a husband's pure love do for his wife? *(verses 26-27)*

3. How are husbands commanded to love their wives? *(verses 28-30)*

4. Verse 31 is quoted from Genesis 2:24. This was and is God's original design for marriage. Marriage has always been a picture of God and His relationship with His people (in the Old Testament), as well as Christ and the church (in the New Testament). As believers, why is it so important for our marriages to reflect Christ?

Read Ephesians 5:33 again. God created us and commanded that we provide for each other what He created us to need. He created men to need respect and women to need love. An excellent book on marriage is *Love and Respect* by Dr. Emerson Eggerichs. He provides great insight into every husband's need for respect. Just as husbands are commanded to love their wives unconditionally, wives are commanded to respect their husbands uncondi-

> Without love she reacts without respect. Without respect, he reacts without love. – EMERSON EGGERICHS

tionally. Eggerichs explains, "The Love and Respect Connection is clearly within Scripture, but so is the constant threat that the connection can be strained or even broken. And then came what I call the 'aha' moment: this thing triggers itself. Without love she reacts without respect. Without respect, he reacts without love—ad nauseam."[6]

One of the ways we reflect Christ to a lost world is through our marriages. There is no excuse for "falling out of love." Love is not a noun to describe what you are feeling; it is a verb to describe how you are behaving. We choose to love because God loves us and we desire to please Him in how we imitate Him.

C. S. Lewis said,

But of course, ceasing to be "in love" need not mean ceasing to love. Love in this second sense—love as distinct from "being in love"—is not merely a feeling. It is a deep unity, maintained by the will and deliberately strengthened by habit; reinforced by [in Christian marriages] the grace which both partners ask, and receive, from God. . . . "Being in love" first moved them to promise fidelity: this quieter love enables them to keep the promise. It is on this love that the engine of marriage is run: being in love was the explosion that started it.[7]

Evaluate your role as a wife. Are you pleasing the Lord? If you have been struggling in your marriage, seek the Lord and ask Him to restore the feelings of love. Until the feelings return, choose to do what you know is right: Offer your husband unconditional respect, knowing God will bless your efforts.

In his book *Sacred Marriage*, Gary Thomas said, "Don't run from the struggles of marriage. Embrace them. Grow in them. Draw nearer to God because of them. Through them you will reflect more of the spirit of Jesus Christ. And thank God that he has placed you in a situation where your spirit can be perfected."[8]

FURTHER THOUGHTS:

DAY THREE

A DIRECTIVE FOR FAMILY AND WORKPLACE RELATIONSHIPS

Ephesians 6:1-9

PAUL FOCUSED NOT ONLY on the relationships within a marriage but also on other relationships most people experience at one time or another—that of children and parents, and employees and employers.

> **Key Point:**
>
> Everyone should submit to authority.

Read Ephesians 6:1-4. The Greek word for *obey* in verse 1 is *hupakouo*. It means "obey, give heed, follow, yield."[9] It is the same word used in verse 5 in reference to slaves and masters.

Read the parallel verse in Colossians 3:20. It is imperative that we teach our children to obey. If we begin with consistent rules and discipline when our children are toddlers, we will have a much easier time when they are teenagers. Just like in all relationships, children need to know they are loved. If they feel secure in your love they will be more likely to obey.

But this passage goes beyond outward obedience and requires that children honor their parents (verse 2). Honor is a heart issue. Children can be obeying on the outside but dishonoring their parents on the inside. This lack of honor will eventually surface through attitudes and behavior.

1. This commandment was the first one to be given with a promise. What is the promise? *(verse 3)*

2. Why are fathers instructed not to provoke their children to anger or exasperate them? *(verse 4)*

3. What are fathers instructed to do? *(verse 4)*

If you have children in your home, ask yourself these questions:

- Are our rules age-appropriate?
- Is discipline consistent and timely?
- Is our home a place of peace—a refuge from the world?

4. **Read Titus 2:3-5.** The older and more mature women are to teach the younger women. What were the first two things listed that they were to teach?

I have now moved into the role of "older woman." (I don't think I can deny it now that my own children are having children.) What about you? How are you using your knowledge of God's Word and your life experiences to encourage the next generation?

All of us have someone who is younger and less experienced than we are. If you are not currently intentionally teaching or discipling someone, begin to ask the Lord to put someone in your life so you will have the opportunity to obey this Scripture. After praying about it, write the person's name here: _____.

Now begin to pray about how and when you will fulfill this obligation.

Read and compare Ephesians 6:5-9, Colossians 3:22-24, and 1 Peter 2:18-21.

5. How do these passages relate to the employer and employee? How should they shape our behavior in the workplace?

6. Make a list of attitudes and actions that should be evident in our lives. *(Ephesians 6:5-6)*

7. How are we to live? *(verse 7)*

8. We must operate in the workplace with the awareness that we answer to a Master who is much higher than our boss or the company through which we have our employment (verses 8-9). How will being aware that God is watching you and will reward your behavior change your work ethic?

We must teach and model respect for authority in all areas of our lives. If we come home from work complaining about our boss and being disrespectful in front of our children, we cannot expect them to show respect for those in authority over them.

> To serve one's employer well is to serve Christ well. — JOHN MACARTHUR

Remember, submission is actually an outward manifestation of our trust in God. He has commanded it, and when we obey He will bless our obedience.

FURTHER THOUGHTS:

DAY FOUR

PRACTICAL APPLICATION

Ephesians 5:22–6:9

Read Ephesians 5:22–6:9 again. Did you discover any benefits of being in Christ as you read? Record them on your "Benefits in Christ" chart on page 30.

> **Key Point:**
>
> Our relationships should reflect Christ!

Look at Ephesians 5:33 as translated in The Amplified Bible:

However, let each man of you [without exception] love his wife as [being in a sense] his very own self; and let the wife see that she respects and reverences her husband [that she notices him, regards him, honors him, prefers him, venerates, and esteems him; and that she defers to him, praises him, and loves and admires him exceedingly].

1. On a separate piece of paper, list the ten ways you can respect your husband as stated in this passage. Put the list in your Bible. Begin to pray over this list. Ask the Lord to enable you to obey His Word. I challenge you to begin doing these things for at least two weeks. You will be shocked at the response of your husband. You might just begin to "fall in love" all over again!

2. Now consider your other relationships. In what ways can you better reflect Christ in each of the following relationships that apply to your life?

   a. As a child:

   b. As a parent:

c. As an employee:

d. As an employer:

Yes, it is difficult to love your spouse. But if you truly want to love God, look right now at the ring on your left hand, commit yourself to exploring anew what that ring represents, and love passionately, crazily, enduringly the fleshly person who put it there. It just may be one of the most spiritual things you do. — GARY THOMAS

FURTHER THOUGHTS:

SESSION 7 LISTENING GUIDE

REFLECT!

Ephesians 5:22–6:9

It is not so much that you trust your husband will hear from God but that God is big enough to lead your husband without your interference. Your greatest influence, as a woman, is submission and prayer.

—IVA MAY

WE MUST BE FILLED with the Spirit to model Christlike behavior in all of our relationships. It will take the continual filling of the Spirit (on a daily and sometimes moment-by-moment basis) for us to please Christ in our daily lives.

1. **Spirit-Filled Marriage** *(5:22-33)*

A submissive wife—unconditional respect for her husband

A loving husband—unconditional love for his wife

The imitation of Christ—see Philippians 2:5-11

2. **Spirit-Filled Parenting** *(6:1-4)*
Obedient children
   It's a matter of the heart.
Disciple-making parents:

- Bless your children
- Instruct your children
- Discipline your children
- Pray for, with, and over your children

3. **Spirit-Filled Employees and Employers** *(6:5-9)*
Employees should honor authority.

- Work as unto the Lord.
- Work for eternal reward.

Employers should respect their employees.
We are all equal in Christ.

Recommended Reading:
Love and Respect by Emerson Eggerichs
Sacred Marriage by Gary Thomas

STAND!

Ephesians 6:10-24

Finally, be strong in the Lord and in the strength of His might. Put on the full armor of God, so that you will be able to stand firm against the schemes of the devil. For our struggle is not against flesh and blood, but against the rulers, against the powers, against the world forces of this darkness, against the spiritual forces of wickedness in the heavenly places.

—Ephesians 6:10-12

UP TO THIS POINT in the book of Ephesians, Paul laid the foundation for standing firm against the Enemy. He realized that we must understand our position in Christ before we can walk in the Spirit. Subsequently, we must be walking in the Spirit in order to be able to stand firm against the Enemy. Each foundational truth is dependent upon the preceding truth. Here in the final verses of Ephesians we discover how to stand firm against Satan and his schemes.

Day 1: The Adversary *(Ephesians 6:10-12)*
Our fight is against Satan.

Day 2: The Weapons *(Ephesians 6:13-20)*
We must put on the armor of God.

Day 3: The Closing *(Ephesians 6:21-24)*
We conquer the Enemy through love.

Day 4: Practical Application *(Ephesians 6:10-24)*
We are to stand!

THE ADVERSARY

Ephesians 6:10-12

And finally, although we are seated above the enemy, we are in an ever present warfare. Some skirmishes are worse than others; the war's not over. So, we need to stand firm in the Lord, put on the whole armor of God so we can resist the devil.

— KAY ARTHUR

Key Point:

Our fight is against Satan.

THROUGHOUT THE BOOK OF Ephesians, Paul was completely candid about the reality of sin in the world. The culture of his day was one that condoned, and often even promoted, sin. And ours is no different. The Christian life is not easy. We face temptations coming at us from many directions. We struggle with sin, and we struggle in our relationships. But Paul didn't just leave it at that. In chapter 6, he made it very clear that our struggle is not against flesh and blood but against the Enemy of our souls, and he instructed us how to stand firm in our faith.

Read Ephesians 6:10-12.

1. How are we strengthened to stand against the Enemy? *(verse 10)*

2. In verse 11 we are told to "put on the full armor of God." This command indicates that it is the believer's responsibility to appropriate the weapons that God has provided. How do you "put on" the armor?

The detailed description of the armor (given in verses 14-17) may stem from Paul's close proximity to a Roman soldier while in prison awaiting trial (see also Acts 28:16,20).[1]

3. Who or what is our struggle against? *(verse 12)*

The Bible Knowledge Commentary gives us some insight into the evil forces we struggle against:

> Though the ranks of satanic forces cannot be fully categorized, the first two (rulers and authorities) have already been mentioned in [Ephesians] 1:21 and 3:10. Paul added the powers of this dark world (cf. 2:2; 4:18; 5:8) and the spiritual forces of evil. Their sphere of activity is in the heavenly realms, the fifth occurrence of this phrase, which is mentioned in the New Testament only in 1:3, 20; 2:6; 3:10; 6:12. Satan, who is in the heavens (2:2) until he will be cast out in the middle of the Tribulation (Rev. 12:9-10), is trying to rob believers of the spiritual blessings God has given them (Eph. 1:3).[2]

So we know who our Enemy is, but do we really *know* him? Do we know what he's like? When you're in a battle, you must know your enemy. Just as opposing teams in sports study their opponents, you must be able to recognize yours. Military regiments study not only their opponents but also the terrain upon which they will be meeting them. We need to know who Satan is. He is called by many names in Scripture, and those names tell us many things about him.

4. List the names for Satan used in the following verses:

a. Genesis 3:1; Revelation 12:9

b. Matthew 4:3

c. John 8:44

d. 2 Corinthians 4:4

e. 2 Corinthians 11:13-15

f. Ephesians 2:2

g. 1 Peter 5:8

h. Revelation 12:7-11

Satan is our enemy, but we must remember that his power is not equal to God's. We are often tempted to think that Satan has more power than he actually does and that he is able to do things only God can do. In *The Bible Exposition Commentary*, we read:

> Many students believe that in the original Creation, he (Satan) was "Lucifer, son of the morning," (Isa 14:12-15) and that he was cast down because of his pride and his desire to occupy God's throne. Many mysteries are connected with the origin of Satan, but what he is doing and where he is going are certainly no mystery! Since he is a created being, and not eternal (as God is), he is limited in his knowledge and activity. Unlike God, Satan is not all-knowing, all-powerful, or everywhere-present.[3]

This passage in Ephesians lets us know that we are up against a very real and hostile Enemy. He is organized, and His goal is destruction. But we must never equate his power with God. And we must also not equate humans with Satan.

It is imperative for us to understand that we do not struggle with people. Our struggle is very clearly a spiritual one. Consequently, we are wasting our time fighting people when instead we need to be resisting the Devil. When

> Unlike God, Satan is not all-knowing, all-powerful, or everywhere-present.
> – *THE BIBLE EXPOSITION COMMENTARY*

Paul was in Ephesus there was a riot (see Acts 19:21-41). Demetrius and his associates instigated the riot against Paul. But it was actually the spiritual powers that opposed the gospel that were using Demetrius and the others to come against Paul.

So how do we enter into this spiritual battle and operate from the victory Christ purchased for us? We need to understand what God has provided for us through His armor and His Word. We must also understand that our Enemy is a formidable one, and the only way we can resist him is from our position and our covering in Christ.

FURTHER THOUGHTS:

DAY TWO

THE WEAPONS

Ephesians 6:13-20

IN VERSES 10-12, PAUL identified our Enemy. In the following verses, he used a military metaphor of a soldier's armor to explain how to protect ourselves and fight against that Enemy. For it is a fight, and we must always be prepared for it.

Read Ephesians 6:13-20.

1. Verse 13 tells us once again to "stand firm." In verses 14-17 we read the descriptions of the various pieces of God's armor. Fill in the following chart with the pieces of armor and their corresponding spiritual components.

Piece of Armor	Spiritual Component

2. Which of the pieces of armor do you feel you use the best?

3. Which pieces do you need to use better?

There is no question that we must be ready for Satan to attack at any time. We won't get a warning, so we must put on our armor daily. The *Women's Evangelical Commentary* puts it clearly: "Satan will not wait for the Christian to get his act together and dress for battle; he will start his attack when you are most vulnerable."[4] It is the times when we feel the least like fighting that we most need to be wearing God's armor.

> Satan will not wait for the Christian to get his act together and dress for battle; he will start his attack when you are most vulnerable. – *Women's Evangelical Commentary*

4. How are we are to pray? *(verse 18)*

Paul knew that prayer was the key to the battle with the Enemy. Let's take a look at John Calvin's thoughts about the place of prayer in spiritual warfare and in life:

> Having put armour on the Ephesians, [Paul] now enjoins them to fight by prayer. This is the true method. To call upon God is the chief exercise of faith and hope; and it is in this way that we obtain from God every blessing. . . . He exhorts them to persevere in prayer, when he says *with all perseverance.* For by this he tells us that we must press on cheerfully, lest we faint. With unabated ardour we must continue our prayers, though we do not immediately obtain what we desire.[5]

It is easy to stop praying when we don't see the answers or when things seem to be going well, but we cannot quit! Without prayer we will not be able to stand firm in our spiritual battles. We must continue praying in faith and remember that God has already won the ultimate battle with Satan. We will have momentary troubles, but in the end, the Enemy will not prevail.

5. What did Paul ask his readers to pray for him? *(verses 19-20)*

Isn't it amazing that even though Paul was in prison when he wrote this letter, he didn't request for prayers that he would be released from prison but instead asked for prayers that he might proclaim the gospel with boldness? How many times have we been in difficult circumstances and instead of seeing them as an opportunity for sharing the gospel, we instead focus on our discomfort and fleshly desire for relief at all costs? Is it possible to miss divine appointments because we are so shortsighted?

FURTHER THOUGHTS:

DAY THREE

THE CLOSING

Ephesians 6:21-24

AS WAS TYPICAL OF Paul, he closed his letter to the Ephesians with some personal greetings, instructions, and final thoughts on the themes of the letter. It is often tempting to skip over these final verses, but it is in these personal words that we can see Paul's true heart for the church and for his Lord.

Key Point:

We conquer the Enemy through love.

Read Ephesians 6:21-24.

1. What message was Tychicus to take to the apostles? *(verses 21-22)*

2. What three spiritual qualities are mentioned? *(verse 23)*

    a.

    b.

    c.

      Paul closed his letter to the Ephesians the same way he opened it—by asking for peace and grace for his brothers and sisters in Christ.

3. In the final verse of Ephesians, Paul mentioned a special kind of love. What word was used for this kind of love? *(verse 24)*

> Good-bye, friends. Love mixed with faith be yours from God the Father and from the Master, Jesus Christ. Pure grace and nothing but grace be with all who love our Master, Jesus Christ. – EPHESIANS 6:23-24 (MSG)

This imperishable love is the kind of love described in 1 Corinthians 13 that "bears all things, believes all things, hopes all things, endures all things" and never fails (verses 7-8). It is this love that will ultimately conquer our Enemy. As we love the Lord with all of our heart, soul, mind, and strength, we will love others as we love ourselves (see Mark 12:29-31).

It is as we surrender to this amazing love that we are motivated and empowered to stand! empowered to stand!

FURTHER THOUGHTS:

DAY FOUR

PRACTICAL APPLICATION

Ephesians 6:10-24

Key Point:

We are to stand!

WE HAVE BEEN GIVEN weapons that enable us to stand against the schemes of the Enemy. Our Father has given us everything we need to live as more than conquerors, and that begins with God's Word. We read in *The Beginner's Guide to Spiritual Warfare*, "The first of the weapons is the Word of God. This is the truth that nullifies the effect of Satan's primary tactic of deception. . . . It is the Word that is the 'sword of the Spirit' (Ephesians 6:17). It is especially the Word as appropriated by us and spoken with trust and confidence."[6]

It is vitally important to know God's Word. Please consider selecting an accountability partner and ask her to check with you to see how you're doing with your personal Bible study and Scripture memorization. You will find that the Holy Spirit will bring verses to mind when you are praying about a decision or when you encounter an attack from the Enemy.

Then incorporate God's Word into your prayer life. There is nothing more powerful than to pray the Word of God. In John 15:7-8 Jesus said, "If you abide in Me, and My words abide in you, ask whatever you wish, and it will be done for you. My Father is glorified by this, that you bear much fruit, and so prove to be My disciples." Did you notice that Jesus said His words were to abide in us? When we pray from His place of abiding—the very words of God—then we know He will answer our prayers. Verse 8 says "by this," which means by answered prayer the Father is glorified. And not only is He glorified, but we also prove by this that we are His disciples.

1. How has the Lord answered prayer in your life recently? Has He given you His Word to pray in a specific situation or for a specific individual?

We must not confide in the armor of God, but in the God of this armor, because all our weapons are only mighty through God.
— WILLIAM GURNAL

God has given us everything we need for life and godliness. Appropriate His provision in the name of Jesus through the power of the Spirit. Bear much fruit and glorify our Father. May we be found faithful—standing firm—when we see Him face-to-face!

FURTHER THOUGHTS:

SESSION 8 LISTENING GUIDE

STAND!

Ephesians 6:10-24

There is a visible and an invisible world that intersect, and we live in the intersection. A cosmic conflict is raging, and it has eternal implications. The souls of men and women, of little boys and girls, of people of every nationality and color and language all over the planet are at stake. The enemy seeks to blind us all to the truth, to dull our souls and ruin our lives. That's what spiritual warfare is all about.

—CHIP INGRAM, *THE INVISIBLE WAR*

1. **Empowered to Stand** *(verses 10-11)*
   Ephesians 1:18-23

   Ephesians 3:20

2. **Our Adversary—Satan** *(verse 12)*
   We must know our Enemy's names.

   We must know our Enemy's goal.

3. **Our Weapons—Armor** *(verses 13-17)*
Belt of truth

Breastplate of righteousness

Shoes of the gospel of peace

Shield of faith

Helmet of salvation

Sword of the Spirit

4. **The Battle—Prayer** *(verses 18-20)*
Why do we pray?

How do we pray?

5. **The Result—Love Incorruptible** *(verses 21-24)*
Grace and peace

A final word: Be strong with the Lord's mighty power. Put on all of God's armor so that you will be able to stand firm against all strategies and tricks of the Devil. For we are not fighting against people made of flesh and blood, but against the evil rulers and authorities of the unseen world, against those mighty powers of darkness who rule this world, and against wicked spirits in the heavenly realms.

—EPHESIANS 6:10-12 (NLT)

NOTES

INTRODUCTION

1. Lawrence O. Richards, *The Teacher's Commentary* (Wheaton, IL: Victor, 1987), 913.

SESSION 1: BLESSED!

1. Thomas C. Brisco, *Holman Bible Atlas* (Nashville: Broadman, Holman, 1998), 255.
2. Warren Wiersbe, "Ephesians 1:7," *The Bible Exposition Commentary* (Wheaton, IL: Victor, 1996).
3. Charles Caldwell Ryrie, *Ryrie Study Bible* (Chicago: Moody, 1978), 1780.
4. A. W. Tozer, *The Knowledge of the Holy* (San Francisco: Harper, 1961), 29.
5. Ryrie, 1780.
6. Gary Thomas, *Holy Available* (Grand Rapids, MI: Zondervan, 2009), 71.
7. John Piper, *Let the Nations Be Glad: The Supremacy of God in Missions* (Grand Rapids, MI: Baker, 1993), 26.

SESSION 2: ALIVE!

1. Warren Wiersbe, "Ephesians 2:4," *The Bible Exposition Commentary* (Wheaton, IL: Victor, 1996).
2. Dorothy Kelley Patterson and Rhonda Harrington Kelley, eds., *Women's Evangelical Commentary: New Testament* (Nashville: Broadman, Holman, 2006), 542.
3. Wiersbe.
4. Elvina M. Hall, "Jesus Paid It All," 1865.
5. Gary Smalley, "Free Personality Test," *The Smalley Family Official Site*, http://smalley.cc/marriage-assessments/free-personality-test.
6. *Life Application Study Bible* (Wheaton, IL: Tyndale, 1997), 964.
7. Helen H. Lemmel, "Turn Your Eyes Upon Jesus," 1918.

SESSION 3: UNCONTAINABLE!

1. John MacArthur, *The MacArthur New Testament Commentary* (Nashville: Thomas Nelson, 2007), 613.
2. Stephen D. Renn, ed., *Expository Dictionary of Bible Words* (Peabody, MA: Hendrickson Publishers, 2005), 659.
3. John Calvin, *Calvin's Commentaries: The Epistles of Paul the Apostle to the Galatians, Ephesians, Philippians and Colossians*, trans. T. H. L. Parker (Grand Rapids, MI: Eerdmans, 1965), 161–162.
4. Watchman Nee, *The Release of the Spirit* (New York: Christian Fellowship Publishers, 2000), 12.

SESSION 4: WALK!

1. A. W. Tozer, *The Pursuit of God* (Camp Hill, PA: Christian Publications, 1982), 90.
2. R. C. Sproul, ed., *The Reformation Study Bible* (Orlando: Ligonier Ministries, 2005), 1711.
3. Dorothy Kelley Patterson and Rhonda Harrington Kelley, eds., *Women's Evangelical Commentary: New Testament* (Nashville: Broadman, Holman, 2006), 554.
4. Oswald Chambers, *My Utmost for His Highest* (Grand Rapids, MI: Discovery House, 1995), September 25.
5. All definitions taken from *Zondervan NASB Exhaustive Concordance* (Grand Rapids, MI: Zondervan, 2000) or Spiros Zodhiates, ed., *Hebrew-Greek Key Word Study Bible* (Chattanooga, TN: AMG Publishers, 1990).

SESSION 5: CHANGED!

1. Richard Foster, *Celebration of Discipline* (San Francisco: Harper, 1988), 8.
2. John Ensor, *The Great Work of the Gospel* (Wheaton, IL: Crossway, 2006), 126–127.
3. John MacArthur, *The MacArthur New Testament Commentary* (Nashville: Thomas Nelson, 2007), 605.
4. Nancy Leigh DeMoss, *Holiness* (Chicago: Moody, 2004), 81.
5. Francis Frangipane, *The Three Battlegrounds* (Bethesda, MD: Arrow Publications, 1989), 21.

SESSION 6: IMITATE!

1. E. K. Simpson and F. F. Bruce, *The New International Commentary on the New Testament: The Epistles to the Ephesians and Colossians* (Grand Rapids, MI: Eerdmans, 1979), 114.

2. John MacArthur, *The MacArthur New Testament Commentary* (Nashville: Thomas Nelson, 2007), 607–608.

3. Simpson and Bruce, 115.

4. Dorothy Kelley Patterson and Rhonda Harrington Kelley, eds., *Women's Evangelical Commentary: New Testament* (Nashville: Broadman, Holman, 2006), 560.

5. Warren Wiersbe, "Ephesians 5:19," *The Bible Exposition Commentary, Vol. 2* (Wheaton, IL: Victor, 1996).

SESSION 7: REFLECT!

1. Spiros Zodhiates, ed., *Hebrew-Greek Key Study Bible* (Chattanooga, TN: AMG, 1990), 1884.

2. Lawrence O. Richards, *Bible Reader's Companion*, electronic ed. (Bellingham, WA: Logos, 1996), 802.

3. John MacArthur, *The Fulfilled Family* (Nashville: Thomas Nelson, 2005), 43.

4. Gary Thomas, *Sacred Marriage* (Grand Rapids, MI: Zondervan, 2000), 13.

5. Lawrence O. Richards, *The Teacher's Commentary* (Wheaton, IL: Victor, 1987), 931.

6. Emerson Eggerichs, *Love and Respect* (Nashville: Thomas Nelson, 2004), 6.

7. C. S. Lewis, *Mere Christianity* (San Francisco: Harper, 1952), 109.

8. Thomas, 133–134.

9. Zodhiates, 1883.

SESSION 8: STAND!

1. John F. Walvoord and Roy B. Zuck, eds., *The Bible Knowledge Commentary* (Wheaton, IL: Victor, 1983), 2:643.

2. Walvoord and Zuck, 2:643.

3. Warren Wiersbe, "Ephesians 6:10," *The Bible Exposition Commentary* (Wheaton, IL: Victor, 1996).

4. Dorothy Kelley Patterson and Rhonda Harrington Kelley, eds., *Women's Evangelical Commentary: New Testament* (Nashville: Broadman, Holman, 2006), 569.

5. John Calvin, *Calvin's Commentaries: The Epistles of Paul the Apostle to the Galatians, Ephesians, Philippians and Colossians*, trans. T. H. L. Parker (Grand Rapids, MI: Eerdmans, 1965), 221.

6. Neil T. Anderson and Timothy M. Warner, *The Beginner's Guide to Spiritual Warfare* (Ventura, CA: Regal, 2000), 140.

ABOUT THE AUTHOR

DONNA GAINES, MEd, is a devoted student of God's Word who has written and taught Bible studies for the past twenty years. She has an intense desire to see women not only study God's Word but also be changed by it.

Donna's first book, *There's Gotta Be More*, was published by B&H Publishing Group and released in 2008. Donna served as the editor of the *One-Year Women's Devotional*, published by NavPress. She also writes a monthly women's column for *Delivered*, a Christian/family publication.

Donna is married to Steve Gaines, pastor of Bellevue Baptist Church in Memphis, Tennessee. They have four children and three grandchildren.

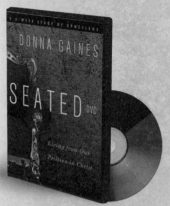